ISRAEL-PALESTINE

FOR CRITICAL THINKERS

ISRAEL-PALESTINE

FOR CRITICAL THINKERS

RICHARD BASS

Information on how to obtain copies of this book is available at:

Web site: www.forcriticalthinkers.com

Design and Layout: BlueApple*Works* Inc.

Developmental Editing: Jamie Bush

Photo Credits:

123RF.com: © Peter Spirer (p 112 inset)

Courtesy of Freedom House (p 114)

Creative Commons: François-Joseph Navez (p 9); Webscribe (p 10); Steven G. Johnson (p 15 top); CNG (p 18); David Germain-Robin (p 25); Gryffindor (p 29 top); Ynhockey (p 35 top); p 37; Bundesarchiv, Bild 146-1987-004-09A / Heinrich Hoffmann / CC-BY-SA (p 58); Government Press Office (p 67, p 70, p 90); Jewish Agency for Israel (p 68 bottom); p 72 (top); Ilan Bruner (p 72 bottom); Willem van de Poll (p 76); Israel Defense Forces (p 96 main and inset, p 98 inset); tomer.gabel (p 97 top); Aaron Vazquez (p 98); Natan Flayer (p 100-101 top); beivushtang (p 106); p 108 (bottom); Davidmosberg (p 111); RossFrenett (p 115); Kw0 (p 116)

Dreamstime.com: © Anticiclo (p 19 top); © Noam Armonn (p 29 bottom)

Library of Congress: American Colony Jerusalem Collection (p 13, p 27 top, p 42); pg 33, G. Eric and Edith Matson Photograph Collection (p 60)

Map Illustrations (all): Joshua Avramson

Public Domain: Heinrich Bünting (p 4); Osmar Schindler (p 12); James Tissot (p 16); Gustave Doré (p 17); Valentin de Boulogne (p 20); Myrabella (p 21); Aert de Gelder (p 24); Dominique Papety (p 26); M. Strayamsky (p 29 top inset); Bernard Picart (p 29 inset); pg 33 (inset); Talmoryair (p 34 top); Avraham Soskin (p 34 top inset); p 34 bottom; p 35 botom; Ullstein Bilderdienst, Berlin (pg 38 inset); Henri Meyer (p 38); Carl Pietzner (p 39 top); p 39; p 40; p 41; John Collier (p 44); p 47; p 48; Molnár József (pg 49); William Orpen (p 50); p 52; Edward N. Jackson (US Army Signal Corps) (p 55); p 56 (main and inset); The Palmach Archive (p 57); Rudi Weissenstein (p 64); p 65; p 66; Fred Csasznik (p 67 inset); Kluger Zoltan (p 68 top, p 80); p 68 (top inset); p 70 (inset); John Phillips (p 77); p 82 (inset); CIA (p 82, p 83); David Falconer (p 83 inset); White House Staff Photographers (pg 84); Sharon Farmer (p 93); B. Železnik (p 94 top); Paul Morse (p 94 bottom); p 97 (inset); Alex Catalan (p 100 bottom); Europecentral (p 101 bottom); Fred Csasznik (p 107 bottom); U.S. Department of State (p 108); National Photo Archive Israel (p 109);

Shutterstock.com: © Boris-B (p 5 left); © kavram (p 5 right top); © Rostislav Glinsky (p 5 right bottom, p 95, p 113, p 118); © AridOcean (p 6); © Creativemarc (p 7 left top); © Noam Armonn (p 7 right top); © maxmacs (p 7 middle right, left); © Michal Ninger (p 7 right bottom); © kavram (p 7 left bottom); © Bzzuspajk (p 15 bottom); © Joseph Calev (p 19 inset); © shahreen (p 22); © OPIS Zagreb (p 23); © Ioannis Ioannou (p 27 bottom); © ChameleonsEye (p 28, p 78, p 79, p 112, p 117); © ayazad (p 30); © wideweb (p 31); © istanbul_image_video (p 32); © Karol Kozlowski (p 36); © Ryan Rodrick Beiler (p 86, p 92); © Morten Normann Almeland (p 88); © Protasov AN (p 102); © Konstantnin (p 110)

ISBN: 978-0-9918186-2-4

Printed in USA

ACKNOWLEDGEMENTS

THIS PROJECT HAS BEEN MADE POSSIBLE
THROUGH THE SUPPORT OF:

MR. PINI AND MRS. COLETTE AVITAL

MR. MICHAEL AND MRS. MARSHA LAX

TABLE OF CONTENTS

PART ONE

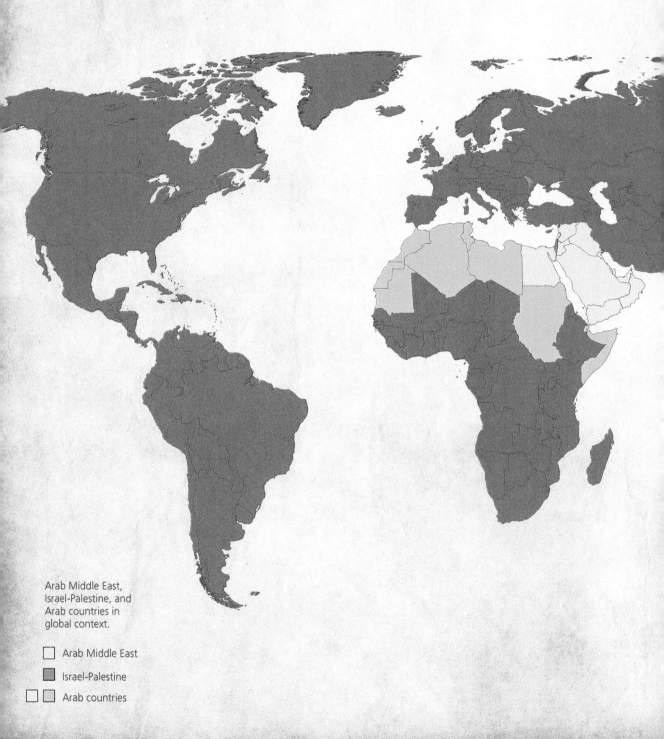

Arab Middle East,
Israel-Palestine, and
Arab countries in
global context.

☐ Arab Middle East

■ Israel-Palestine

☐ ■ Arab countries

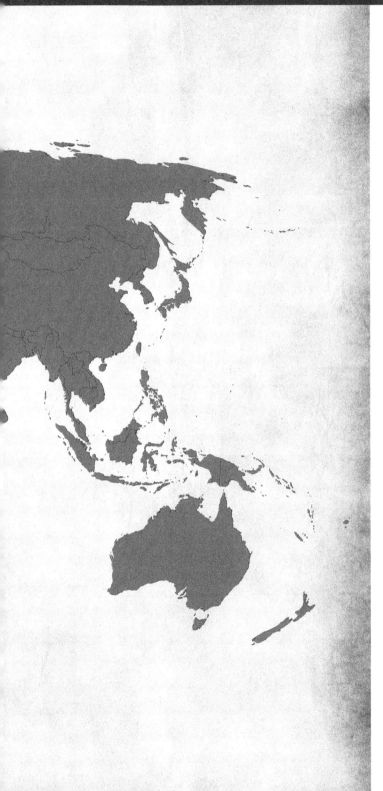

IT IS A NARROW STRIP OF TERRITORY, NOWHERE MORE THAN 80 MILES ACROSS, BOUNDED BY THE MEDITERRANEAN SEA TO THE WEST AND THE JORDAN RIVER AND THE ARABIAN DESERT TO THE EAST. IT IS THE SOUTHWESTERN EXTREMITY OF A SWATHE OF LAND, SOMETIMES KNOWN AS THE FERTILE CRESCENT, THAT CURVES UP AND AROUND FROM THE PERSIAN GULF TO THE SINAI PENINSULA. IT SITS IN THE WESTERN-MOST PORTION OF WHAT WE REFER TO TODAY AS THE MIDDLE EAST. "MIDDLE" REFERS TO ISRAEL-PALESTINE'S POSITION RELATIVE TO THREE CONTINENTS: EUROPE, AFRICA, AND ASIA.

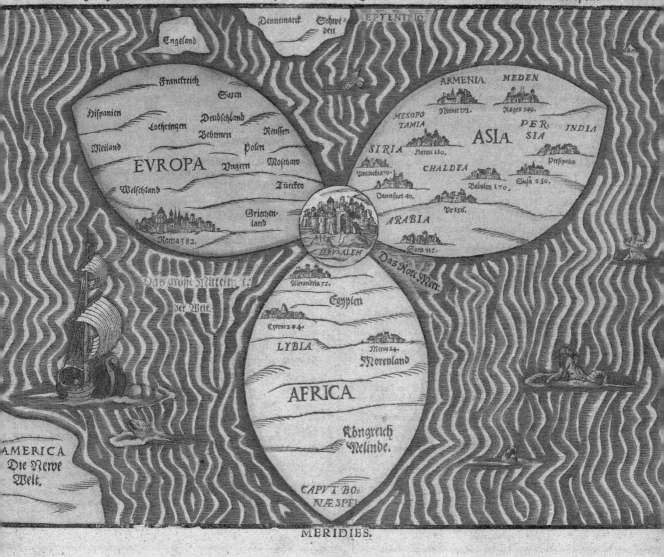

Die gantze Welt in einem Kleberblat/Welches ist der Stadt Hannouer meines lieben Vaterlandes Wapen.

The Bünting Map, published in 1581, is a historic illustration of the world. The three continents of the Old World are shown divided by the seas, but connected by Jerusalem — the hub of the world because of its religious importance.

It is a land that has gone by various names. English ones include Israel, Canaan, the Promised Land, the Holy Land, Judea and Samaria, and Palestine. The first of these names—Israel—is derived from the name given to the biblical Patriarch Jacob, whose descendants became the Israelites. The last one, Palestine, is derived from the name of one of its ancient occupants: the Philistines. This was the name the Romans gave to the land around the second century CE to replace the name Judea, and it was taken up by the post-Roman empires of Europe and Islam. We will refer to this land as Israel-Palestine.

This land's importance in human history is out of all proportion to its size. Many millennia ago, Israel-Palestine saw the dawn of human civilization, and it has since played a central role in the story of humanity. It is sacred to the three great monotheistic religions of the world, Judaism, Christianity, and Islam. Collectively, these religions are followed by more than half the peoples on earth.

4

The Abrahamic religions, Judaism, Christianity, and Islam, consider Jerusalem a holy city. Each of these religions has sacred sites there. (Clockwise from left: Church of Holy Sepulchre, Western Wall, and Dome of the Rock.)

Israel-Palestine's story is an ancient one. In the West (and especially in North America), 250 years is considered a long time. It is longer, for example, than the United States of America has existed as a nation. The history of human civilization in Israel-Palestine, by comparison, dates back many thousands of years. The actors in this ancient story include the most powerful world empires of the past—the Egyptians, Assyrians, Babylonians, Persians, Greeks, Romans, and Ottomans. The most recent chapter concerns the modern State of Israel.

Today, Israel-Palestine is a land coveted by two peoples, Arabs and Jews. The conflict between their national aspirations, ongoing now for almost a century, has caused much hardship on both sides. Each side subscribes to versions of the past that support their respective territorial claims. We can't hope to understand the problems in this region without knowing the actual history.

Some people refer only to recent and current events when explaining the problems now facing the Middle East. A more complete understanding of what's happening today must start thousands of years ago, when the land was called Canaan.

A COMPLETE UNDERSTANDING OF WHAT'S HAPPENING TODAY MUST START THOUSANDS OF YEARS AGO, WHEN THE LAND WAS CALLED CANAAN.

BEFORE THE ISRAELITE CONQUEST: 1800–1250 BCE

CANAAN IN THE SECOND MILLENNIUM BCE

The physical position and the topography of Israel-Palestine have profoundly shaped its history. In the ancient world, Canaan was a point of intersection between different peoples and worlds. Its geographical position made it a natural corridor between Asia and Africa. To the west, the Mediterranean opened to the civilizations of the Aegean world. Nomadic tribes of the Arabian desert populated the region's eastern edge. Canaan was a major transit area and junction for trade. Caravans crisscrossed the coun-

Canaan's geographical position made it a natural corridor between Asia and Africa. The area of Canaan, as described in the Bible, roughly corresponds to modern-day Lebanon, Israel, Gaza, The West Bank, the western part of Jordan, and southwestern Syria.

try carrying goods between the Nile Valley and the Euphrates, as well as to Arabia and the busy Mediterranean seaports of Phoenicia.

The topography within Canaan promoted variety in its inhabitants, and its population was not a single nation but an ethnic patchwork of peoples. The terrain was unusually diverse for such a small area. From west to east, the land changes dramatically. The Mediterranean basin gives way to a mountain ridge in the centre of the country, which in turn drops steeply to the Jordan rift valley. In the north lie the Golan Heights, and in the south is the Negev desert. This division of Canaan into hills and valleys and varied ecosystems naturally produced diversity in the peoples living there. Before the Israelite conquest, Canaan was a land of heterogeneous city-states that were, quite often, fighting amongst themselves.

The lack of political or cultural unity within Canaan left the territory particularly vulnerable to the major powers of the time. Egypt lay to the south, and to the north were the Hittite Empire and the various nations of

Mesopotamia and beyond. Why would these superpowers be interested in this tiny strip of land?

Dominance over Canaan brought great political advantages. Militarily speaking, its geographical location made ancient Canaan strategically important as a bridgehead. Control of it was needed for any attack by one power upon another. That is why this land became an international battleground more often than any other area in the ancient world. From the dawn of human history, then, Canaan was exposed to and periodically dominated by the earliest centers of civilization, which provided a continual stream of settlers into the region. Through the millennia, as we noted above, the ethnic make-up of Canaan became extremely mixed. Before the Israelite conquest and settlement of the land c. 1250-1200 BCE, various peoples, of assorted ethnic and cultural backgrounds, inhabited the land. The ones mentioned in biblical sources include Amalekites, Hittites, Jebusites, and Amorites, as well as Canaanites (Numbers 13:29). Egyptian documentary sources, such as the El Amarna letters, attest to this biblical picture of diversity.

THE PATRIARCHAL PERIOD

The proto-history of Israel, spanning the generations from Abraham to Jacob in the Bible, is known as the Patriarchal period. What we know about it is based partly on the biblical account, partly on the findings of modern scholarship. Extra-biblical sources, documentary and archaeological, tell us that the Bible stories are consistent with demographic and historical conditions of the time.

The Patriarchal period is very relevant to our understanding of current events. The covenantal promises described in the biblical account are crucial to the territorial claims of the peoples now in conflict over Israel-Palestine. In some cases, the adherents of Judaism, Christianity, and Islam interpret these promises differently.

The varied ecosystems of the Canaan region naturally produced diversity in the many peoples living there.

THE BIBLE AS HISTORY?

Many of us are not used to approaching the Bible as a work of history. Is it really a credible source of factual information? Aren't its narratives just myths and folklore that have been passed down for thousands of years?

The prevailing views about this question have shifted back and forth in the last two centuries. Until about 1800, most people took the biblical stories to be literally true. They accepted the Bible as a reliable account of ancient history. This changed in the 19th century, when German textual scholars began to argue that the early biblical narratives were largely myth, no more factual than Greek stories of Hercules. This skeptical view of the Bible prevailed into the first decades of the 20th century. It is still the view of many.

Over the past hundred years, there has been a shift away from this purely skeptical view and a restoring of credit to the biblical account. This change is owing to modern science; it has radically revised our understanding of antiquity. Archaeologists of the last half century, instead of dismissing ancient texts and their stories out of hand, have used them to guide their excavations. In the light of recent decades' discoveries, some of the biblical stories have taken on a fresh historical reality.

This is not to say that everything in the biblical account is historically accurate. The more remote in time the people and events being described, the less clear we become about their historical authenticity. In the Bible's earliest books, espe-cially, we cannot always distinguish legend from historical fact. Where these books are concerned, modern investigators have uncovered circumstantial evidence for some of the events described—places and names, migratory patterns, and customs. But there isn't much evidence concerning specific people and events.

This changes once we get to the later books. The events they describe, including the stories of the ancient Israelite kingdoms, date from around 2,800 years ago. With these books, there is strong direct evidence that the events in the narrative actually occurred. For example, the written records of other empires—the Egyptians, Babylonians, and Assyrians—support the biblical account. The Bible is not a history book. But it contains a great deal of information about ancient history and culture, and some of this information is supported by modern archaeological and documentary evidence.

Whether or not we believe in a literal way the events described in the Bible, the fact remains that the story of Abraham and his descendants is integral to three of the world's great monotheistic religions—Judaism, Christianity, and Islam. As such, this story has altered the course of history and affected millions of people over several millennia. And if our aim is to gain some understanding about how and why Israel-Palestine is significant to Jews, Christians, and Muslims, we need to understand the biblical narrative.

> A SKEPTICAL VIEW OF THE BIBLE PREVAILED INTO THE FIRST DECADES OF THE 20TH CENTURY. IT IS STILL THE VIEW OF MANY.

8

THE BIBLICAL NARRATIVE

The first patriarch described in the Bible is Abraham. According to the biblical account, Abraham received a divine directive to go from his home in Haran (northwestern Mesopotamia) to the land of Canaan—that is, present day Israel-Palestine. There, according to scripture, God made a covenant with Abraham. He promised to give the land to Abraham and his descendants, and in return the Israelites were to worship God alone and to obey his laws. The notion that God gave the Land of Canaan to the Israelites is a basic tenet of Judaism. In Judaism, the nation (or people), the Bible, and the land are all connected.

When Abraham received this promise, he had no heirs. The Bible tells us that he was 85 years old, and his wife Sarah 75. Sarah assumed she was too old to bear children. Following the custom of the time, she offered her handmaiden Hagar to Abraham, so that Abraham could produce an heir. Hagar gave birth to a son named Ishmael.

Shortly afterwards, Sarah herself gave birth to a son named Isaac. As the boys grew older, Sarah became concerned about inheritance rights and demanded that Abraham send Hagar and Ishmael away. According to the biblical account, Isaac was Abraham's rightful heir, and the land of Canaan was his legacy. Isaac is the second biblical patriarch.

In the biblical narrative, Isaac's son Jacob becomes the third biblical patriarch. Jacob is renamed Yisrael (Israel) after his struggle with a divine being. This is the source of the name Israel. Jacob's twelve sons were called B'nei Yisrael, which literally means "the Children of Israel." In the Bible, the descendants of Jacob's twelve sons become the ancient Israelites.

ABRAHAM IN JUDAISM, CHRISTIANITY, AND ISLAM

Jews, Christians, and Muslims alike accept Abraham as a prophet and consider Ishmael and Isaac to be the patriarchs of the Arab and Jewish people, respectively. The casting-out of Hagar and Ishmael is the point in the story where the Judeo-Christian narrative diverges from the Islamic one. According to Islamic tradition, Abraham did not cast Ishmael out. Rather, God ordered him to take Hagar and Ishmael to Mecca, where Abraham later returned, with Ishmael, to build the Ka'aba—the most sacred shrine of Islam. Muslims turn in its direction when praying.

Where the biblical events of the patriarchal period are concerned, history and legend are not always distinguishable. But the biblical account stands as a remarkably complete and detailed record, unique for its time, of an ancient people's coming into being. One eminent scholar of Jewish history has observed that

> of no people in the biblical period other than Israel has there been preserved such a detailed account of its proto history or, certainly, such a complete and continuous description as is to be found in the patriarchal narrative and in the Exodus-Conquest cycle.

A depiction of Hagar and Ishmael in the desert by François-Joseph Navez. Ishmael is recognized by Muslims as the ancestor of several prominent Arab tribes and as the forefather of Muhammad.

ISRAELITE CONQUEST AND SETTLEMENT OF CANAAN c.1225 BCE

The biblical story tells us that the descendants of the twelve tribes went from Canaan to Egypt, and then, led by Moses, they emerged from bondage there. The Israelites' aim, after leaving Egypt, was to claim the territorial inheritance promised to their ancestor—the first patriarch, Abraham. This eventually led to their conquering and settling Canaan. This phase of Israelite history and the legendary events involved, which are a cornerstone of Judaism, occurred in the 13th century BCE, according to biblical chronology.

Epigraphic material and archaeological evidence support the notion that during the 2nd millenium BCE West Semitic peoples of Mesopotamia, ancestors of the Israelites, were migrating to Canaan and in some cases continuing on from there to Egypt. Some of these Semitic immigrants to Egypt, like the biblical Joseph, rose to positions of power. Others lived as slaves and indentured labourers, hauling stones for the imperial pyramids. The historical picture these sources provide is consistent with the biblical narrative.

Larger geopolitical developments during this period affected the ancient Israelites. Extra-biblical sources tell us that, in the late-13th century BCE, a power vacuum had begun to develop in Canaan, as the power of Egypt declined. The region had been

The Merneptah Stele, also known as the Israel Stele (13th century BCE), was discovered in 1861 by English egyptologist Sir William Matthew Flinders Petrie.

firmly under Egyptian control for many centuries, but now it was being contested by the Hittite empire to the north. Canaan became a primary battleground in the struggle between these powers. Each side was assisted by numerous subordinate allies, including the independent city-states of Canaan.

Archaeological evidence tells us that one of the allies involved in this imperial conflict was Israel. The Egyptian pharaoh Merneptah conducted a military campaign in Canaan sometime during his decade-long reign (1213–1203 BCE). This campaign produced an artifact called the Merneptah Stele, which bears inscriptions on its stone surface. The stele records Merneptah's boasting of his military victories over various Canaanite nations. One of them is named Israel. This is the first recorded extra-biblical mention of Israel.

The Israelite conquest of Canaan began toward the second half of the 13th century BCE, with the world of the Middle East in flux. The recession of Egyptian authority in Canaan allowed nomadic and semi-nomadic tribes from the eastern border areas, including the Israelites, to gain a foothold in the region. Over the next two centuries, the Israelites ultimately became the dominant people in Canaan.

The Bible tells us that the territory the Israelites conquered was divided among twelve tribes. The tribe of Judah—the descendants of Jacob's oldest son—received the largest portion of land and settled in the southern part of the territory. The remaining Israelite tribes received portions that extended northward and eastward into modern-day Lebanon, Syria, and Jordan.

Following the Israelite settlement of Canaan, there was a long period of strife between the Israelite tribes and the neighboring Canaanite peoples. There was also conflict with the Philistines.

MEDITERRANEAN SEA

TYRE

ARAM

ASHER
NAPHTALI
EAST MANASSEH
ZEBULUN
ISSACHAR
WEST MANASSEH
AMMON
DAN
EPHRAIM
GAD
BENJAMIN
REUBEN
JUDAH
SIMEON
MOAB
EDOM

Map of the area settled by the Twelve Tribes of Israel according to the Book of Joshua.

■ Non-Israelite communities

THE PHILISTINES IN CANAAN

Goliath, or Goliath of Gath (one of five city states of the Philistines), was a giant Philistine warrior. According to the biblical narrative, he was defeated in single combat by David, the future king of the Israelites.

A major factor in the instability of late-13th-century Canaan was the Sea Peoples' arrival in the Levant. Who were the Sea Peoples? They were powerful fighting nations from the Aegean region in the Mediterranean.

One of the groups of Sea Peoples was the Philistines. They became a formidable adversary to the ancient Israelites, as described in the Bible. The Philistines were not a national state headed by a single ruler, but a confederacy of city-states. According to the findings of modern archaeology, they initially ruled the coastal city-states of Gaza, Ashkelon, and Ashdod, which they were able to conquer as Egyptian control in the region weakened. The Bible refers to a number of battles between the Israelites and various Philistine powers, one of which involves the famous story of David and Goliath. The Philistines disappeared from history following the Babylonian conquest c.586 BCE, but their name lived on.

THE ORIGINS OF THE NAME "PALESTINE"

The name "Palestine" is derived from the Hebrew term *Plishtim*—Philistines, in English—which was the biblical name for one of the Sea Peoples who invaded and settled the southern coastal area of Canaan at the beginning of the Iron Age (around 1187 BCE).

After the Assyrian conquest in the last quarter of the 8th century BCE, the coastal area they had settled was referred to as *Philistia* and then *Palaestina*. The Romans, after quelling the second Jewish rebellion in 135 CE, replaced the name *Judea* with the Latinized name *Syria-Palaestina* in an attempt to eradicate the ancient Israelite connection with the territory and discourage future Jewish uprisings.

When the Arabs conquered the area in the name of Islam in the 7th century, they called it *Filastin*, the Arabic equivalent of Palaestina. Over the centuries, the English name for *Palaestina* and *Filastin*—that is, Palestine—appeared on Western maps of the region and in literature concerning it.

After the British defeated the Ottoman Empire in World War I, the mandate they received from the League of Nations to administer the area was called the Mandate for Palestine.

Herbert Samuel, a Brittish official, arrived in Palestine on June 20 1920 to take up his appointment as the first High Commissioner of Palestine. Samuel was the the first Jew to govern the historic land of Israel in nearly 2000 years.

ISRAELITE KINGDOMS: 1000–720 BCE

The discord among the Israelite tribes in Israel-Palestine ended with the monarchy of King David, which began in approximately 1000 BCE. Under him, there was a unified Israelite kingdom. He brought the Philistine threat to a close through military force as well as negotiation.

King David conquered the Canaanite city of Jebus, named it Jerusalem, and made it the capital of the Israelite kingdom. In the Bible, Jerusalem is frequently called Zion. It was in Jerusalem, in about 964 BCE, that King Solomon, David's son, built the first Jewish Temple.

After the death of Solomon, the Israelite kingdom split into two. Ten of the twelve tribes formed a northern kingdom called Israel. The two southern tribes became the Kingdom of Judah, with Jerusalem as its capital. The Assyrians destroyed the northern Kingdom of Israel in approximately 720 BCE. The Israelites survived, however; the Kingdom of Judah remained. Assyrian inscriptions from this period make reference to the Israelite kingdom. They also make reference to an Arab chief.

ARABS IN THE ANCIENT WORLD: 9TH CENTURY BCE

The first known extra-biblical reference to Arabs is an inscription on one of the Kurkh monoliths. These are stone monuments, dating from 853 BCE, that commemorate the reigns of two Assyrian kings. The monolith concerned with one of these kings—Shalmaneser III—includes a description of his victory at the Battle of Qarqar. One of the conquered kings listed on the monolith is "Gindibu the Arbaa." (The Kurkh monolith also lists Shalmaneser's victories over two ancient Israelite kings mentioned in the Bible: Ahab and Jehu.)

Who were the Arabs? *Arbaa* is the Assyrian term for the people who lived in the *arabah* (desert). The He-

THE DISCORD AMONG THE ISRAELITE TRIBES IN ISRAEL-PALESTINE ENDED WITH THE MONARCHY OF KING DAVID, WHICH BEGAN IN APPROXIMATELY 1000 BCE.

Bas-relief showing Jehu, king of Israel, bowing before the Assyrian King Shalmaneser III.

brew term *aravah* and the Arabic term *arabah* refer to the desolate and dry areas of the Jordan rift valley in the eastern part of Israel-Palestine and to other desert regions of the Middle East. The *aravah* was home to nomadic tribes whose lifestyle and culture were shaped by their environment. These nomadic tribes also lived in the desert regions of the Arabian Peninsula and in parts of Syria. The Arabs in the ancient world were not a distinct nation or people who identified themselves as such. *Arab* was an umbrella term, used to designate the various tribes who dwelt in the deserts of the Middle East.

In a later reference to the Arabs of the ancient world, the biblical books of Nehemia and Second Chronicles list a person called "Geshem the Arvi" (*arvi* is the biblical adjective derived from the noun *aravah*) among those who opposed Nehemiah. Nehemiah was the leader of the Jewish effort, in the 5th century BCE, to rebuild the walls of Jerusalem after the Babylonian conquest.

Arabs today are a highly heterogeneous collection of peoples, with various ancestral origins and identities. They primarily inhabit Western Asia, North Africa, and parts of the Horn of Africa.

BABYLONIANS, PERSIANS, AND THE FIRST JEWISH DIASPORA 586–430 BCE

In 586 BCE, the legendary Babylonian king Nebuchadnezzar invaded the Kingdom of Judah and destroyed Jerusalem and Solomon's Temple. Many of the Israelite people, including its leaders and its scholars, were taken to Babylon (modern-day Iraq). This event is known as the diaspora (from the Greek word for "scattering, dispersion").

In 536 BCE, 50 years after the first Jewish diaspora, the Persians defeated the Babylonians, and the Persian King Cyrus permitted the Jewish exiles to return to their former kingdom in Judah. Many remained in Babylon. There, over the millennia, they established communities and distinguished academies of learning. The Jews that returned to Judah, led by biblical figures Ezra and Nehemia, rebuilt the walls of Jerusalem and built a Second Temple on the site of the original one.

The Edict of Cyrus the Great authorized the exiled Jews to return to Judah and rebuild their Temple. The Cyrus Cylinder, currently housed in the British Museum, is an artifact memorializing Cyrus's policies.

The first significant Jewish Diaspora was the result of the Babylonian Exile of 586 BCE. After the Babylonians conquered the Kingdom of Judah, part of the Jewish population was deported into slavery.

THE DESIRE TO RETURN TO ZION

The desire to return to Zion—to Jerusalem and the land of Israel—has been expressed in daily Jewish prayers since the days of the Babylonian exile 2500 years ago. Psalm 137 is probably the best known expression of the Jewish people's desire to return:

By the rivers of Babylon,

There we sat down,

Sat and wept,

As we remembered Zion.

These words have even become part of contemporary pop culture, adapted to music and lyrics in the 1970s by a Jamaican reggae group and subsequently popularized in Europe and North America by the band Boney M.

The word *Zion*—a synonym in Jewish literature both for Jerusalem and for the entire Land of Israel—appears in the Bible over 100 times.

Depiction of Nehemiah viewing the ruins of Jerusalem's walls after his return from Babylon. The Jewish community of Babylon included Nehemiah and Ezra the Scribe, whose return to Judea in the late 6th century BCE is associated with significant changes in Jewish ritual observance and the rebuilding of the Temple in Jerusalem.

THE ISRAELITES AND THE GREEK AND ROMAN EMPIRES: 332 BCE–135 CE

Over the next centuries, the territory of Judea was the scene of ongoing Israelite struggles against the ancient Greek and Roman empires and their polytheistic ideologies. Initially, both the Greeks and Romans gave the ancient Israelites a fair measure of autonomy in Israel-Palestine. Under Alexander the Great, for instance, the Jewish communities were governed by their own body of religious law.

Under Alexander's successors, however, the Israelite communities began to face harsher decrees and bans on religious freedom. Eventually, the ancient Israelite communities revolted under the Hasmoneans (Macabbees) and regained their autonomy. This autonomy remained strong in the region until the Romans delivered two crushing blows to the Jewish people in the first two centuries of the Common Era.

The first of these blows came in 70, when Titus, the son of the emperor Vespasian, ended a four-year battle with the Jews by destroying Jerusalem and the Second Jewish Temple. The Arch of Titus in Rome commemorates this Roman victory; its engravings show Jewish Temple artifacts being carried away as the

The *Judaea Capta* coins were struck for 25 years under Vespasian and his two sons who succeeded him as Emperor—Titus and Domitian. These commemorative coins were issued in bronze, silver, and gold by mints in Rome, throughout the Roman Empire, and in Judaea itself.

The Arch of Titus is a Roman triumphal arch which commemorates Roman victories in the Jewish War in Judaea. One panel (inset) shows the victory procession with the participants carrying booty from the Temple of Jerusalem after the sacking of the city.

spoils of war. The Romans also minted coins, inscribed with the phrases "Judea capta" and "Judea divicta," to celebrate their victory. Some of these coins survive today. The second blow to the Jewish people in Israel-Palestine followed their uprising against the Romans in 135 CE, known as the Bar Kokhba revolt. It was crushed by the Emperor Hadrian, and the Roman vengeance that followed was severe. The Romans laid waste to the land of Judea, plowed the site of the Temple, and barred Jews from Jerusalem. They killed hundreds of thousands of Judeans and enslaved or sold into slavery many others.

A second diaspora began, more far-reaching than the Babylonian one; the Jewish people were scattered across the Middle East and into ancient Europe. In an effort to prevent any further Jewish rebuilding or asso-

ciation with the region, the Romans renamed the conquered territory *Syria-Palaestina*. The term *Palaestina*, as we noted above, was associated with the ancient Israelites' former adversaries, the Philistines.

It was during this period of Roman oppression, in the first century CE, that a spiritual teacher, raised according to Jewish tradition, began to teach a new version of biblical monotheism, one that would change the course of history.

THE ROMANS LAID WASTE TO THE LAND OF JUDEA, PLOWED THE SITE OF THE TEMPLE, AND BARRED JEWS FROM JERUSALEM.

RISE OF CHRISTIANITY IN ISRAEL-PALESTINE: 1ST CENTURY CE

Paul is generally considered one of the most important of Jesus's apostles. Today, his epistles continue to be vital roots of the theology, worship, and pastoral life in the Roman and Protestant traditions of the West, as well as the Orthodox traditions of the East.

Jesus is Christianity's central figure. According to Christian theology, the events of his life took place in the 1st century CE, during the time of the Roman occupation of Israel-Palestine. Jesus is believed to have been born around the dawn of the Common Era in Bethlehem, just south of Jerusalem. The facts of his early life are uncertain, but there is general agreement that he was a Jew who was familiar with the Torah and the Law of Moses. In his spiritual teaching, he incorporated Torah precepts, the most fundamental of which is monotheism. The Christian New Testament, particularly the Gospels, recounts the major events of Jesus's life. These took place in the Galilee, in northern Israel-Palestine (Samaria), and in Judea. According to Christian scripture, Jerusalem and the surrounding area were the site of the Last Supper and of Jesus's arrest, trial, Crucifixion, burial, and resurrection.

After Jesus's death, it was Paul, a Jewish convert to the new religion who never physically met Jesus, who carried the message of Christianity to Rome and to various parts of the Roman Empire. Paul was active around the middle of the first century of the Common Era. Largely through his efforts and influence, Christianity underwent tremendous growth in the first and second centuries.

By the year 64, some two years after the death of Paul, Christianity had become widespread in Rome. But the Roman emperors of the time, Nero and Domitian, saw the new religion as a political threat and outlawed it. The course of Christianity could have ended there. Instead, something remarkable happened in 312 that led to Christianity's being established as the official state religion of the Roman Empire.

What happened was the conversion to Christianity of Constantine I. He was the emperor of Rome from 306 to 337. The motives behind Constantine's conversion were likely political and pragmatic rather than spiritual. Nonetheless, his conversion contributed greatly to the spread of the faith and helped transform the Roman province of Palaestina into a Christian Holy Land.

In 326, Constantine's mother Helena, a fervent Christian, visited Jerusalem. During her visit, she tried to locate Christianity's sacred sites—for example, the sites of Jesus's crucifixion and burial. As a result of her findings new structures were eventually built in Jerusalem, the most important being the Church of the Holy Sepulchre. According to Christian theology, this is where Jesus was crucified, where he was buried, and where he will be resurrected. The name of the Holy City was also changed from Aelia Capitolina—the name the Romans had given it after the second Jewish rebellion, in 135 CE—back to Jerusalem.

Christianity dominated in Israel-Palestine until the 7th century CE, when Islam rose to power and took control of the region.

Constantine—as the first Christian emperor—is a significant figure in the history of Christianity. The Church of the Holy Sepulchre, built on his orders at the purported site of Jesus's tomb in Jerusalem, became the holiest place in Christendom.

AFTER JESUS'S DEATH, IT WAS PAUL, A JEWISH CONVERT TO THE NEW RELIGION, WHO CARRIED THE MESSAGE OF CHRISTIANITY TO ROME AND TO VARIOUS PARTS OF THE ROMAN EMPIRE.

THE BIRTH OF ISLAM: 7TH CENTURY CE

Mecca is regarded as the holiest city in the religion of Islam. Pilgrimage to it, known as the *Hajj*, is obligatory for all able Muslims. Mecca is home to the Ka'aba, Islam's holiest site. Pilgrims circumambulate the Ka'aba seven times to show their submission to Islam.

According to Islamic tradition, Muhammad, the founder and prophet of Islam, was born in the small oasis town of Mecca in western Arabia, in 571 CE. Muhammad was a merchant. He was familiar with the local Jewish people and their religion, which may explain the similarities between Judaism and Islam (dietary laws, fasting, daily prayer).

Islamic tradition tells us that in the year 610, when he was 40 years old, Muhammad received his first revelation and began preaching. His following and influence increased rapidly. Not everyone was supportive of his teaching, however; Muhammad faced resistance from the polytheistic tribal culture of Mecca and was eventually forced to leave.

In the year 622 CE, Muhammad set up the first community of his followers in the town of Yathrib, later named Medina. The migration of Muhammad and his followers from Mecca to Medina is known in Arabic as the *hijra*. It marks the first year of the Islamic calendar and the beginning of Islam's rise in history.

Ten years after leaving Mecca, Muhammad returned with an army and conquered the city. Mecca is the location of the holiest site in Islam, the Ka'ba. According to Muslim belief, this is the House of God built by Abraham and Ishmael. It is the main reason that Mecca is the holiest city in Muslim tradition, and it is the direction (or *qibla*) that all Muslims face when praying.

At the time of his death in 632, Muhammad had established Islam in most of the Arabian Peninsula. After his death, his successors, called caliphs, rapidly expanded the empire their prophet had begun to found. Within a couple of decades, the Arab Islamic empire included virtually all of

the Middle East, as well as the Persian Empire (modern-day Iran) and most of the Roman Byzantine Empire.

Israel-Palestine was under Islamic rule from the 7th century, when Arab Muslims conquered the region, until the end of the 11th century, when Latin Crusaders invaded. During this span of nearly 400 years, Jewish and Christian communities remained in Israel-Palestine under Islamic dominion.

ISLAM, JERUSALEM, AND THE TEMPLE MOUNT

Among the caliph Omar's late-7th-century conquests was the city of Jerusalem. The Arabs call the city *al-Quds*. Although Jerusalem itself is not mentioned by name in the Qur'an (the Islamic holy book), it was the original qibla chosen by Muhammad (before he changed it to the Ka'aba, in Mecca). The caliphate gave the city sacred status and constructed the Dome of the Rock on the Temple Mount.

The Temple Mount may be the most contested piece of real estate on earth. It is extremely significant to Jews, Christians, and Muslims because of the religious traditions regarding it, especially the rock inside the Dome. In Judaism and Christianity, the rock is associated with the Foundation Stone from which Jews and Christians believe the earth was created. It is also revered as the site of Abraham's test with Isaac.

According to Muslim belief, the Dome of the Rock is the site to which Muhammad journeyed from Mecca. The rock itself is the place from which he ascended to heaven during his Night Journey, as the Qur'an describes in Sura 17. Collectively, these beliefs make the al-Haram al-Sharif—as the Temple Mount is known to Muslims—the third holiest site in Islam after Mecca and Medina. It is the site of the al-Aqsa Mosque, constructed in the late 7th and early 8th centuries.

The Temple Mount is the most prominent place in the Old City of Jerusalem. The Dome of the Rock and the Al-Aqsa Mosque, standing atop the site of the former Jewish temple and above Christianity's holiest sites, reflect the Muslim notion that Islam has replaced Judaism and Christianity as the true religion.

The Dome of the Rock is located at the visual center of a platform known as the Temple Mount. It was constructed on the site of the Second Jewish Temple, which was destroyed during the Roman Siege of Jerusalem in 70 CE.

REPLACEMENT THEOLOGY

The concept of the Covenant is central to Judaism and to the history of the ancient Israelites. This was the formal agreement between the Israelites and God, first made under Abraham and later renewed under Moses. It meant that the Israelites were to worship God alone and to obey his laws. In return, they were promised the land of Canaan (Israel-Palestine). Some Christians and many Muslims believe that the Jews have been replaced as the chosen people and that the Covenantal promises have been passed to their own religions, respectively. There are different versions of replacement theology, and they vary in their premises.

Christians who believe in replacement theology hold that they are the true inheritors of God's Old Testament promises to Israel. They believe that the Covenant with Jesus has superseded the Mosaic Covenant, making Christians, not Jews, the chosen people. Many Christians do not accept this school of thought because it ignores St. Paul's New Testament assurance to the Jewish people that God has not rejected them.

Muslims' replacement theology likewise involves a belief that they, not the Jews, have become the true inheritors of God's Old Testament promises. A unique feature of Islamic replacement theology is its wholesale appropriation of Jewish and Christian prophets. Muslims believe that Abraham, Moses, and the later Hebrew prophets (for example, David and Solomon) are prophets of Islam. Jesus, too, is considered a prophet of Islam. The Muslim concept of replacement is a cornerstone of Islamic claims to the Promised Land and a key to understanding the Middle East conflict.

Abraham is revered in three major world faiths, Judaism, Christianity and Islam. In Judaism he is considered to be the original party to the Covenant, the special agreement between the Jewish people and God.

THE LATIN KINGDOM: 1099–1291

Toward the end of the 11th century, Europeans launched the first of many Christian Crusades to take the Holy Land back from the Muslims. They were successful in 1099. Their victory led to the establishment of the Latin Kingdom in Israel-Palestine. Archaeological evidence of Latin Crusader presence has been found on many sites in Israel-Palestine.

At its height, in the mid-12th century, this Christian kingdom roughly encompassed the territory of modern-day Israel and the southern parts of Lebanon. The Crusaders massacred both Jews and Muslims in the course of their conquest.

THE CRUSADERS MASSACRED BOTH JEWS AND MUSLIMS IN THE COURSE OF THEIR CONQUEST.

Belfort Castle was a Crusader fortress located in Southern Lebanon. Saladin captured it in 1190.

RETURN OF ISLAMIC RULE: 1187–1917

THE MAMELUKES AND THE FALL OF THE LATIN KINGDOM

The Latin Church maintained control of Israel-Palestine from 1099 until 1187, when Saladin, almost entirely re-captured the land, including its greatest prize: Jerusalem. The Mamelukes, Muslims from a variety of ethnic backgrounds who served as military slaves under Saladin, eventually rose to become a powerful warrior class and, in some regions of the Middle East, seized political control from their masters. For example, they ruled as sultans in Egypt and Syria from the mid-13th century to the beginning of the 15th century. Their conquest of the Crusader city of Acre, in 1291, marked the conclusive end of the second Latin Kingdom and the end of Christian rule in Israel-Palestine.

The Mamelukes controlled Israel-Palestine for the nearly 300 years, fighting off several Mongol invasions during the 13th and 14th centuries. Many Arabs moved west during this period, fleeing the Mongols. As a result of this migration, Arab Muslims in the 13th century began to form a majority in Israel-Palestine for the first time.

The Siege of Acre (also called Acco) took place in 1291 and resulted in the loss of the Crusader-controlled city of Acre to the Muslims. It is considered one of the most important battles of the time period.

THE OTTOMAN EMPIRE IN ISRAEL-PALESTINE: 1517–1917

At the beginning of the 16th century, the Ottoman Empire conquered the Levant and in the process took Israel-Palestine from the Mamelukes. The Ottoman Turks, the last of the great Islamic empires, had sovereignty in the area until they were defeated by the Allied Powers in World War I.

After the war, the Allied Powers gave to the Arab people the Ottoman Empire's former territories, today called Saudi Arabia, Syria, Lebanon, Jordan, and Iraq. During the same period, they granted Israel-Palestine to the Jewish people. It is these two peoples, the Arab and the Jewish peoples, that are in conflict today in Israel-Palestine.

The Ottoman surrender of Jerusalem to the British forces took place on December 9th, 1917.

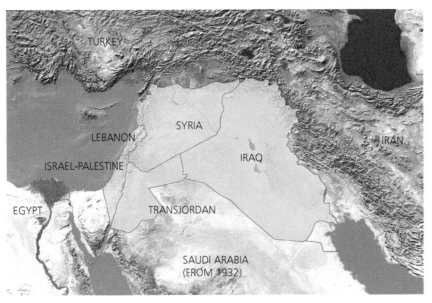

Ottoman territories given to Arabs and Jews after WWI, showing modern borders.

ISRAEL-PALESTINE: FROM ANCIENT ROOTS TO THE 20TH CENTURY

THE JEWISH AND ARAB PEOPLES

Today, the territory of Israel-Palestine is populated by a wide range of ethnic groups. Within this diverse population, two peoples predominate: Arabs and Jews. Who are they?

JEWISH PEOPLE

The Jewish people trace their ancestry to the West Semitic peoples of Mesopotamia, who migrated to Israel-Palestine (Canaan) during the second millennium BCE. A particular group of these people became the ancient Israelites, whose story is related in the Bible. Subsequently, they became the Jews.

For thousands of years, from the biblical era until the Romans crushed the Jewish rebellion in 135 CE, the Jewish people existed as a nation in Israel-Palestine.

After the Roman diaspora, which dispersed the Jews of Israel-Palestine across three continents, the Jewish people continued to function and to self-identify as a people, or nation. They maintained their own language, calendar, philosophical world view, traditions, and academies of learning. For most of their history, the Jews have defined themselves as a people and a nation, not merely as a religious group. The religion of Judaism was only one facet of a nationalistic Jewish identity.

In the 18th and 19th centuries, with the rise of European nationalism, the term "Jewish" narrowed and became a religious designation. During this period, the peoples of Europe began to conceive of themselves in terms of a national identity, based on their place of birth and residence. Responding to this trend, the Jewish people living in European countries began to identify themselves in dual terms, as citizens of a particular country—France or Germany, for example—who followed the Jewish religion.

The Jewish people, owing to the diaspora, lack some of the elements that usually define a people. In particular,

Today, the territory of Israel-Palestine is populated by a wide range of ethnic groups. Citizens of the State of Israel constitute a multicultural population that includes Arabs from across the Middle East and Jews from all over the globe.

Timeless Jewish wedding rituals include a *ketubah* (marriage contract) which is signed by two witnesses, a wedding canopy (*chuppah*), a ring owned by the groom that is given to the bride under the canopy, and the breaking of a glass.

they do not live in close geographical proximity to one another. However, their "peoplehood" has other bases, including the following:

- *Ceremonial chain of tradition.* For thousands of years, generations of Jews have recited the same prayers and followed the same rituals in celebrating the Sabbath, Passover, the Jewish New Year, and the Day of Atonement. Jewish communities around the world have observed the same traditions surrounding key life events, such as marriage and death, since before the Common Era. All of these ceremonial traditions and prayers incorporate a common language: Biblical Hebrew.

- *Chain of Jewish learning and transmission.* Jewish scripture and literature record the names of hundreds of Jewish leaders, sages, and teachers from each of the over one hundred generations spanning the four millennia of Jewish history. Many of these figures are survived by their stories and teachings, and many of their gravesites are found in Israel.

- *Shared experiences and consciousness.* Other bases of Jewish national identity, or peoplehood, are the persecutions they have endured in

common, their persistent self-identification as Jewish, and their ancient attachment to the land of Israel-Palestine, which, according to the Torah, was bestowed on them by God.

Bound by these features, the Jewish people are more consciously a people and a nation than are many of the peoples of the world.

Today, the Jewish people number approximately 14 million and represent about 0.2 percent of the world's population. The State of Israel is home to over 6 million Jews, who make up roughly 75 percent of Israel's citizens. The remainder of the Israeli population comprises a wide range of ethnic, cultural, and religious backgrounds. The largest minority group, making up 20 percent of the total population, are Arab Muslims. A small minority are Arab Christians.

The Jewish people celebrate Passover to commemorate their liberation over 3,300 years ago by God from slavery in ancient Egypt, and their freedom as a nation under the leadership of Moses.

ARAB PEOPLE

The term "Arab" has broadened over time owing to the spread of Islam. In its ancient usage, Arab was the general term applied to the various tribes who dwelt in the deserts of the Middle East. The Hebrew term *aravah* and the Arabic term *arabah*, from which the term *Arab* is derived, refer to the desert. "Arab" did not refer to a particular nation, or people. Today, the term Arab has lost its ancient associations with the desert and now applies to the various 350 million Arabic-speaking peoples that live in the 22 Arab states of the Middle East and North Africa.

The *Arab* people are predominantly Muslim, but Islam is a worldwide religion, and the majority of Muslims are not Arabs. There is a strong association between the Arab people and Islam because the Arabian Peninsula is where Islam originated—Muhammad was born into an Arabian tribe—and because the Qur'an is written in Arabic, which is the religion's lingua franca.

With the rise of Islam in the 7th century, the language and culture of the Arab people spread across the Middle East through Islamic conquest, and Arabic became the dominant language of the Islamic world. It was during this period that the term *Arab* began to take on a broader meaning.

In the 19th century, Arab nationalism arose, along with many other nationalist movements around the world, including Zionism. This was when the Arabs first began to seek emancipation from Turkish rule and to conceive of an autonomous pan-Arab state in the Middle East. After the Allied Powers' victory in World War I, they granted the Arabs prospective sovereignty, through the mandate system, over most of the Middle East.

PALESTINIAN ARABS

The notion of the Palestinians as a separate and distinct Arab people is a recent one. Palestinian Arab nationalism was a late offshoot of 19th-century Arab nationalism. It emerged in the 1920s, when the clashes between the Zionist settlers and the Arab residents of Israel-Palestine began to intensify.

The formal conception of a Palestinian Arab nation distinct from other Arab nations can be traced to the Palestinian National Covenant (or Charter) of 1964.

The Charter uses the phrase "Palestinian Arab people" several times, and it identifies Palestine, with its original Mandate borders, as "the homeland of the Arab Palestinian people" and as "an indivisible part of the Arab homeland."

The Charter explicitly defines Palestinian identity. It provides that a

The Arab States of the Middle East. The popout image shows the Ka'aba in Mecca, Saudi Arabia.

Middle East Region

Arab States

Israel-Palestine

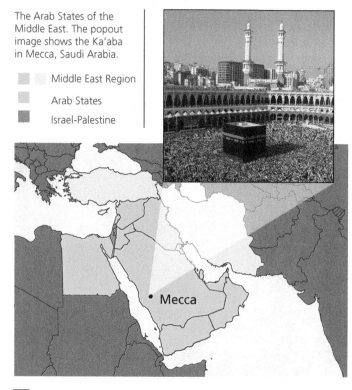

• Mecca

Palestinian is an Arab who was living in Palestine up to 1947 (just prior to the founding of the State of Israel), regardless of when he or she arrived or whether he or she remained in the area after 1947. In other words, any Arabs who came to Israel-Palestine from other Arab lands of the Middle East before 1947—even if they arrived just a few months before and left a few months after—are considered Palestinian under the Charter.

Palestinian identity, as defined by the Charter, also involves a unique patrilineal element. Arabs who left Israel-Palestine and have not returned are considered Palestinian. So—according to the Charter—are their children, grandchildren, and great-grandchildren, even if they were born outside of the region, so long as the father is Palestinian.

Today, there is a significant Arab population in Israel-Palestine. Over 1 million Arabs are living in Israel and citizens of it. They make up over 20 percent of the Israeli population. Judea and Samaria (The West Bank) is also home to over 2 million Palestinians and the Gaza Strip to another 1.5 million.

HOT TOPIC 1.3
ARAB CLAIMS TO ISRAEL-PALESTINE

The Jewish people and the Arab people have now been engaged in a territorial conflict for nearly a century. The dispute concerns which of the two peoples has a stronger claim to Israel-Palestine. The opposing claims have theological and historical components, as well as legal ones.

Arab Muslims believe that their theological claim to the land—and to the Temple Mount in Jerusalem, which is sacred to all three Abrahamic faiths—is stronger than both Jewish and Christian claims. The Palestinian Arabs argue, further, that the Jewish people have no historical or ownership rights to the land. They argue that the Jewish people began coming to Israel-Palestine only in the late 19th century and that their arrival caused the displacement and dispossession of the majority Palestinian Arab population.

After the 13th century, the vast majority of the Jewish people did live outside Israel-Palestine. This continued until late in the 19th century. In the 19th and early 20th centuries, conditions in the Ottoman Empire created an opportunity for the Jewish people to return to Israel-Palestine and for large numbers of Arabs to move there as well.

Within Israeli and Palestinian society, the conflict generates a wide variety of views and opinions. This diversity of opinion reflects the deep divisions which exist not only between Israelis and Palestinians, but also within each society.

IN THE 19TH AND EARLY 20TH CENTURIES, CONDITIONS IN OTTOMAN EMPIRE CREATED AN OPPORTUNITY FOR THE JEWISH PEOPLE TO RETURN TO ISRAEL-PALESTINE AND FOR LARGE NUMBERS OF ARABS TO MOVE THERE AS WELL.

ISRAEL-PALESTINE IN THE LATE-19TH AND EARLY-20TH CENTURIES

The population in Israel-Palestine in the 19th century, as in the rest of the Ottoman Empire, was divided along religious lines and class lines. The ruling community was Muslim. All others had inferior legal and political status.

Within the Muslim community itself there were sharp class divisions. It was similar to the feudal system in Medieval Europe. The majority of the population were Arab *fellaheen* (tenant farmers). They dwelt in villages and eked out a precarious living. They were like the Medieval serfs—basically slaves to the landowning elites, who owned the land and collected taxes for the Ottoman government. Many of the fellaheen lived in the central hill region. Others farmed what arable land there was along the coastal plain and in the north central region of the country.

Historically, Christian and Jewish places of worship in Muslim countries were required to be lower in height and to be less imposing than Muslim mosques.

In the late 19th century, much of the land on the coastal plain was difficult to farm, either sand or marsh. The irrigation structures of centuries past had long since disappeared. So most of this region, with the exception of the area outside the Arab city of Jaffa, where oranges were grown, was sparsely populated and thinly cultivated. Tel Aviv, for example, today Israel's major coastal city, was merely a sand dune in the early years of the 20th century. North of Tel Aviv, swamps, such as the Kabara, the largest swamp on the coastal plain, made agricultural settlement prohibitive.

Arab landowners often lived in distant cities where they were engaged in politics while their tenant farmers eked out a precarious living on landowners' properties.

WITHIN THE MUSLIM COMMUNITY ITSELF THERE WERE SHARP CLASS DIVISIONS. IT WAS SIMILAR TO THE FEUDAL SYSTEM IN MEDIEVAL EUROPE.

33

Early Zionists in Israel-Palestine built their settlements on lands purchased from Arab landowners.

■ Land owned by Jews in 1930

▇ Sparsely populated land allotted for Jewish National Home according to the Palestine Mandate

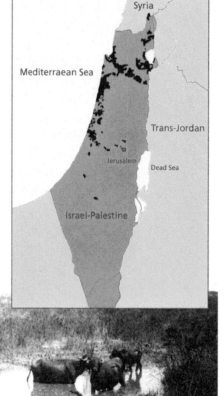

Syria

Mediterraean Sea

Trans-Jordan

Jerusalem

Dead Sea

Israel-Palestine

In the north-central region of Israel-Palestine, the Jezreel Valley—today a green fertile plain covered with fields of wheat, cotton, and sunflowers—was largely devoid of people and cultivated land. It was, for the most part, malarial marshland. In his 1925 report on Palestine, Herbert Samuel, the British government's High Commissioner, gave the following account of the Jezreel Valley as it was in 1920:

> When I first saw it in 1920 it was desolation. Four or five ... Arab villages, long distances apart from one another, could be seen on the summits of low hills here and there.

Firsthand accounts of early-20th-century Israel-Palestine indicate that the focus of the Zionist settlement was desolate terrain such as swamp land—

Malarial swamps, like the Kabara north of present-day Tel Aviv, had to be drained to make early Zionist agricultural settlements possible.

Today, Tel Avi is Israel's financial capital and a major performing arts and business center. Tel Aviv was founded on April 11, 1909. On that day, several dozen families gathered on the sand dunes on the beach outside Yaffa to allocate plots of land for the new city. (inset left)

areas that the Arab tenant farmers avoided as infertile.

The influx of Jewish settlers undoubtedly affected the fellahin, however. Absentee Arab Arab landowners as well as local landowning elites, such as the al-Husseini family, sold extensive tracts of land, and this process dispossessed the tenant farmers to some extent. Some of the fellaheen themselves also sold land. As a result, there were Arab farmers who were left without a livelihood. In some cases, entire Arab villages disappeared because of land sales. The growing population of landless fellaheen had no choice but to move to the urban centres or elsewhere in search of work. Disenfranchised and aggrieved, they would become part of the Arabs' emerging nationalist struggle.

Golda Meir immigrated to Palestine from America and was one of the early pioneers of the Labor Zionist movement. In 1969, Meir became the fourth Prime Minister of Israel.

A PIONEER'S REFLECTIONS

Golda Meir's autobiography *My Life* includes a description of the Jezreel region as it was on her arrival there in 1921. In the following passage, she emphasizes the challenge facing those who sought to reclaim the land:

[Much] of the area consisted of the kind of deadly black swamps that inevitably brought malaria and blackwater fever in their wake. Still, what mattered most was that the pestilential land could be bought, though not cheaply; much of it, incidentally, was sold to the Jewish National Fund by a single well-to-do Arab family that lived in Beirut.

The next step was to make this land arable … .

ISRAEL-PALESTINE: FROM ANCIENT ROOTS TO THE 20TH CENTURY

JEWISH AND ARAB NATIONALISM

The term *Zionism* is derived from the word *Zion,* a frequent synonym in the Bible for "Jerusalem."

The Jewish and Arab nationalist movements emerged more or less simultaneously toward the end of the 19th century, an era of many nationalist movements. Both peoples sought land in the Middle East to achieve their goals, and both turned to the European powers for help. In 1920, in San Remo, a small town on the Italian Riviera, the Allied Powers, with the support of the 51 member states of the League of Nations, set in motion the events that would bring both peoples, Arab and Jews, the right to govern themselves. The lands allocated for the Arab peoples encompassed most of the Middle East. The Jews were to have a small strip of land on the Mediterranean coast. This section will focus on how these movements and decisions came to pass.

POLITICAL ZIONISM

The term *Zionism* is derived from the word *Zion,* a frequent synonym in the Bible for "Jerusalem." Numerous verses in the Bible refer to "Zion" or "Mount Zion" and directly associate Zion with Jerusalem, a city central to Judaism for millennia and mentioned in the Bible over 600 times.

In the 19th century, a Jewish nationalistic movement arose whose aim was to re-establish Jewish sovereignty in Israel-Palestine after nearly 2,000 years. The term *Zionism,* first used in the 19th century, has come to refer primarily to this political and nationalistic aspiration.

ZIONISM AND RELIGIOUS ZIONISM

The desire to return to Zion—to Jerusalem and the land of Israel—has been expressed in daily Jewish prayers since the days of the Babylonian exile 2500 years ago. A longing for Jerusalem and for the Land of Israel is part of Judaism. Judaism does not separate its world view from its concept of nationhood and of a homeland. In Judaism, the Bible, the nation (or people), and the land are all connected. The Land of Israel, then, has always been sacred to religious Jews, a land they believe was promised to them by God and to which they are bound to return with the coming of the Messiah, as foretold in biblical prophecy.

Many religious Jews rejected political Zionism when the movement began. They did so on the grounds that it was a secular, socialist (i.e., atheistic) movement and that an attempt to recover the Land of Israel by human—rather than divine—agency was blasphemous.

Religious Zionists sought to reconcile religious Jews to political Zionism. Led by their chief spokesman, Rabbi Abraham Isaac Kook (1865–1935), they aimed to provide religious legitimation for the political movement. Their justification was as follows: political Zionism, though conceived and led by secular Jews, was not merely a secular phenomenon; it was the tool by which God promoted his scheme of returning world-wide Jewry to the Land of Israel, where they were to establish a sovereign Jewish state in which Jews would live according to the laws of Torah.

Some religious Jews have never been reconciled to political Zionism or to the existence of the State of Israel.

Abraham Isaac Kook was the first Ashkenazi Chief Rabbi of the British Mandatory Palestine. Rav Kook built and maintained channels of communication between the various Jewish sectors, including the secular Jewish Zionist leadership, the Religious Zionists, and non-Zionist Orthodox Jews.

The Growth of Modern Zionism

Until the last decades of the 1800s, the great majority of Jews living in the diaspora (that is, outside Israel-Palestine) foresaw themselves living that way indefinitely. They believed that their future would be assimilation in one form or another. This belief was most firmly rooted in France. The Jews in that country had been emancipated from discriminatory laws and treated as legal equals since 1791. There were similar promising developments all over Western Europe.

Things began to change in 1881. That was when anti-Jewish policies in Russia, under a new anti-Semitic tsar, became extraordinarily oppressive. Jewish communities in that country suffered mob violence, government-organized pogroms, and cruel hardships. The thinking of many late-19th-century Jewish intellectuals underwent a radical shift during this period. They saw what was happening in Russia, and they lost their hopes for assimilation.

In 1894, something happened to accelerate the growth of Zionism in Europe. Known as the Dreyfus affair, it happened in France, a country that many Jews assumed to be a stronghold of tolerance and equal opportunity. Captain Alfred Dreyfus, a Jewish officer in the French army, was falsely accused of selling military secrets to the Germans and was subsequently sentenced to life imprisonment on Devil's Island. He was eventually exonerated and released, but the case revealed the strength of the country's anti-Semitism.

Degradation of Alfred Dreyfus, (inset) on January 5th 1895, as he lost his captain's commission in the French army.

IN 1894, SOMETHING HAPPENED TO ACCELERATE THE GROWTH OF ZIONISM IN EUROPE. KNOWN AS THE DREYFUS AFFAIR, IT HAPPENED IN FRANCE, A COUNTRY THAT MANY JEWS ASSUMED TO BE A STRONGHOLD OF TOLERANCE AND EQUAL OPPORTUNITY.

Among the journalists covering the case was Theodor Herzl (1860–1904), an Austrian Jew. Herzl had grown up, like many European Jews, aspiring to total assimilation. But the injustice of the Dreyfus case and the anti-Semitic mob behavior it inspired in France convinced Herzl of the great vulnerability of the Jews of Europe. In light of the Dreyfus affair, Herzl felt that an independent Jewish state was the only chance the Jews had to survive.

As Herzl saw it, the only solution for Jews worldwide was to emigrate and build a Jewish nation. With this aim in mind, he managed to organize the First Zionist World Congress in Basel, Switzerland in 1897. It marked the birth of Zionism as a political movement. Its stated aim was to create for the Jewish people a legally assured home in Palestine.

After Herzl's early death in 1904, at the age of 44, it was Dr. Chaim Weizmann (1874–1952) who became the leader of the Zionist cause. Weizmann was instrumental in gaining the British government's support for a Jewish state in Palestine.

Theodor Herzl is considered the father of modern political Zionism and, in effect, the founder of the State of Israel. Herzl formed the World Zionist Organization and promoted Jewish migration to Palestine in an effort to form a Jewish state.

In 1906, Weizmann was introduced to Arthur Balfour, an influential English statesman who had previously been prime minister. Weizmann's meetings with Balfour fostered a decade-long political process in England that ultimately resulted in the Balfour Declaration of 1917—Britain's formal expression of approval for the establishing of a Jewish national home in Palestine.

Chaim Weizmann (left) discussing the Palestinian issues with Herbert Samuel (middle) and Lloyd George (right). Weizmann considered the Balfour Declaration the greatest single achievement of the pre-1948 Zionists.

ARAB NATIONALISM

Arab nationalism became a political force around the same time as political Zionism. This movement owed much to the vision and efforts of Husain Ibn Ali, the Sharif of Mecca, and to his son Emir Faisal. Husain was responsible for converting Arab nationalist aspirations into political reality. Like Jewish nationalist hopes, Arab aspirations depended on the support of the European powers, in particular the British government.

BACKGROUNDS OF ARAB NATIONALISM

The origins of Arab nationalism may be traced to mid-19th-century Syria-Lebanon. In the scholarly circles of Beirut, Christian Arab intellectuals began preaching to all Arabs about the need for concord and unity. The idea of unity was foreign to the Arab people, whose culture was individualistic and tribal in nature.

What emerged from these scholarly circles, toward the end of the 19th century, was a common ideal of a united Arab national consciousness. At this time, the regions of the Middle East where Arabs lived were part of

Husain Ibn Ali, was the Sharif of Mecca from 1908 until 1917. He initiated the Arab Revolt in 1916 against the Ottoman Empire during the First World War.

Emir Faisal's delegation at Versailles, during the Paris Peace Conference of 1919. Faisal's original goal was to create an Arab state that would include Iraq, Syria and the rest of the Fertile Crescent.

the Ottoman (in other words, Turkish) empire; the Turks had controlled them for the past four centuries. The nationalist intellectuals called on Syrian Arabs to unite and shake off the Turkish power. The idea of an Arab national consciousness began to spread from Syria into the neighboring Arab-speaking regions.

In June 1913, a series of meetings took place in Paris: this was the First Arab Congress. Among its aims was greater autonomy for the Arab people within the Ottoman Empire. Thus the Arabs, like the Zionists, had begun to organize a nationalist political movement prior to World War I. For the next few years, Arab and Jewish ambitions for statehood, born of quite different impulses, developed side by side. Unfortunately, their ambitions overlapped in one area. The single, unified state that the Arabs envisioned for themselves included the region of Israel-Palestine, which the Zionists also sought.

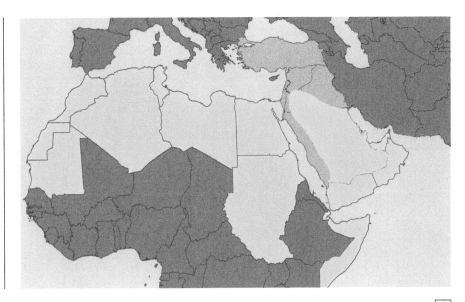

The Ottoman sultanate was abolished in 1922. The majority of the former Sultanate territory was given to Arabs.

- Ottoman Empire in 1914
- Arab World

ISRAEL-PALESTINE: FROM ANCIENT ROOTS TO THE 20TH CENTURY

PART TWO

Austrian troops marching up Mount Zion in 1916.

WORLD WAR I CHANGED THE
COURSE OF HISTORY FOR BOTH THE
ARAB AND THE JEWISH PEOPLES. IT
ULTIMATELY CREATED THE MIDDLE
EAST WE SEE TODAY.

POLITICAL AND LEGAL FOUNDATIONS OF ISRAEL-PALESTINE

WORLD WAR I: PLEDGES AND AGREEMENTS

World War I changed the course of history for both the Arab and the Jewish peoples. It ultimately created the Middle East we see today. By the time the war broke out, the Arab and Jewish nationalist movements were seeking territory to fulfill their aims. The Jews sought Israel-Palestine, and the Arabs sought an area that included the Arabian Peninsula,

Lieutenant Colonel Sir Arthur Henry McMahon was a British diplomat and Indian Army officer who served as the High Commissioner in Egypt from 1915 to 1917.

Mesopotamia (Iraq), and Syria, as well as Israel-Palestine. All of these lands had belonged to the Ottoman Empire for approximately five centuries. They would likely have remained so had it not been for the Great War.

On October 31st, 1914, the Ottoman Empire joined the Central Powers (Germany and the Austro-Hungarian Empire) in the war against the Allied Powers (the British Empire, France, Russia, and their various secondary allies). The Turkish decision increased the significance of the Arab people to the Allies. Why?

The Allied Powers feared that Turkey, the premier Islamic state, would rouse the Arab Muslim world and its tens of millions against them. If Turkey announced that it was at war with the Christian powers of Europe and that the Islamic holy places were in danger, Muslim Arab believers would rally around the banner of the faith.

To prevent this from happening, the Allied Powers looked to ally themselves with the Arabs against the Turks. Their aim in doing so was not only to boost their war effort but to protect their economic interests in the region. This was especially the case for Great Britain, which had vital interests in the Middle East, including the Suez Canal and valuable oil-fields at the head of the Persian Gulf.

The Arab nationalists, for their part, saw that an alliance with the Allied Powers could help them throw off the Turkish yoke and further their goals of Arab independence. Arab nationalists approached the Sharif of Mecca, Husain Ibn Ali—the leading figure in the Arab-Islamic world—with a proposal. They told Husain that they favoured a revolt against Turkey, and they asked him whether he would lead the independence effort. There ensued meetings between Husain's youngest son, Faisal—who was acting as his father's deputy—and six principal Arab leaders. They presented Faisal with a plan of action as well as the terms under which they would agree to cooperate with Great Britain against Turkey. Their plan was to have Husain approach the British with their proposal. Husain agreed to do so, and the Arab leaders pledged to recognize him as the spokesman of the Arab race.

Husain then sent a letter to the British. He told them that he would lead an Arab revolt against the Ottoman Empire in return for an understanding with the British as regards territory. This produced a famous series of letters that have come to be called the McMahon–Husain correspondence.

BRITISH PLEDGES TO THE ARAB PEOPLE

In the course of the McMahon–Husain correspondence, the British pledged territory to the Arab people. During the same period—as we shall see—the British were pledging territory to the

Jewish people. These different pledges came into conflict in the area of Israel-Palestine.

Husain's initial letter to McMahon stated the terms on which the Arab leader was prepared to enter an alliance with Great Britain. Husain demanded that Great Britain recognize the independence of the Arabs in all the territory from the Persian frontier (today's Iran) in the east to the Mediterranean Sea in the west; and from today's northern borders of Syria and Lebanon to the southern tip of the Arabian Peninsula.

In other words, the land Husain requested included the current countries

Map of Husain's territorial demands reflecting his vision of a United Arab kingdom.

Territory requested by Sharif Husain

WAS PALESTINE PLEDGED TO THE ARABS?

The Arabs concluded from the McMahon–Husain correspondence that all of Palestine, including Jerusalem and its Old City, was pledged to them. The British have always denied that this was their intention.

In support of their denial, the British cite the "modification" included in McMahon's response to Husain. McMahon explicitly excluded certain regions from his territorial pledges to Husain. His wording was as follows:

> The districts of Mersin and Alexandretta, and portions of Syria lying to the West of the districts of Damascus, Homs, Hama, and Aleppo, cannot be said to be purely Arab, and must on that account be excepted from the proposed delimitation.

Mediterranean Sea

Adana
Mersin
Urfa
Aleppo
Hama
Homs
Beirut
Acco
Damascus
Baghdad
Jaffa
Jerusalem
Beersheba
Cairo
Basra
Sinai
Persia
Arabian Gulf
Red Sea
Egypt
Indian Ocean

Twenty-five years later, the British government published a report on the controversy over the McMahon–Husain correspondence. Their aim was to adjudicate between the Arab and the British interpretations. Arab representatives as well as British ones were included in the enquiry.

The Arabs concluded the following: "Such geographical description as he [McMahon] and the Sharif give of the portions to be reserved points unmistakably to the coastal regions of northern Syria."

The British representatives, for their part, claimed that McMahon's response to Husain "excluded, and should reasonably have been understood to exclude, the part of southern Syria, consisting of portions of the former Vilayet of Beirut and the former independent Sanjaq of Jerusalem, now known as Palestine." The British also quoted McMahon's views on the matter: "I feel it my duty to state, and I do so definitely and emphatically, that it was not intended by me in giving the pledge to King Husain to include Palestine in the area in which Arab independence was promised."

Map of McMahon's Delimitation of the proposed Arab Kingdom.

· · · · · Western limit to Arab Kingdom proposed by McMahon

of Israel, Lebanon, Syria, Jordan, Iraq, and Saudi Arabia. He wanted this whole region to become one unified Arab State.

McMahon responded. He said that Great Britain was prepared to recognize and uphold Arab independence in all the territory proposed except for portions of land on the Mediterranean coast. He was referring to the region comprising what is now Lebanon and Israel. His wording was indefinite, however. The territories covered in the British pledge were not clearly defined, and this later resulted in much controversy.

British Pledges to the Jewish People

As McMahon and the Sharif of Mecca were exchanging letters, the British government was meeting with representatives of the Jewish people and discussing territorial pledges with them. In 1917, Weizmann, now the president of the Zionist Organization, submitted a proposal to the British government regarding Palestine. The famous declaration that was based on Weizmann's proposal and finally issued by the British government became known as the Balfour Declaration.

The particular wording of the Balfour Declaration was problematic in the long run. It used the phrase "national home," which, unlike the word "state," was unknown in international usage and had no established legitimacy.

The Balfour Declaration (dated November 2nd 1917) was a letter from the British government's foreign secretary Arthur James Balfour to Baron Rothschild, a leader of the British Jewish community. The text of the letter was published in the press one week later, on November 9th 1917.

THE TERRITORIES COVERED IN THE BRITISH PLEDGE WERE NOT CLEARLY DEFINED, AND THIS LATER RESULTED IN MUCH CONTROVERSY.

THE BALFOUR DECLARATION

His Majesty's Government view with favour the establishment in Palestine of a national home for the Jewish people, and will use their best endeavours to facilitate the achievement of this object, it being clearly understood that nothing shall be done which may prejudice the civil and religious rights of existing non-Jewish communities in Palestine, or the rights and political status enjoyed by Jews in any other country.

ISRAEL-PALESTINE IN THE NEW MIDDLE EAST

Arab jurists have sometimes argued that the British had no legal standing to make the Balfour Declaration. Their point is that the territory being pledged was not Britain's to give; in 1917, Palestine still belonged to the Turks.

IF THE BRITISH HAD NO AUTHORITY TO PLEDGE PALESTINE TO THE JEWS, THEN THEY LIKEWISE LACKED THE AUTHORITY TO PLEDGE LAND TO THE ARABS.

But if the British had no authority to pledge Palestine to the Jews, then they likewise lacked the authority to pledge land to the Arabs.

Neither pledge would receive legal weight until after World War I. This process began at the Paris Peace Conference of 1919, when the Jews and the Arabs formally petitioned the Allied Powers for territory. It continued at the San Remo conference in 1920, where the Allied Powers made decisions about the former Ottoman territories.

ZIONIST–ARAB AGREEMENT

On January 3rd, 1919, a significant meeting took place between Chaim Weizmann, head of the Zionists, and the Emir Faisal, the son of the Arab

Emir Faisal I and Chaim Weizmann (left, wearing Arab headdress as a sign of friendship) at their first meeting in June 1918.

leader, Sharif Husain. Just prior to the opening of the Peace Conference, the two men concluded the Faisal–Weizmann Agreement.

This agreement stated that Palestine would become the Jewish national home and would not be included in the proposed Arab state. It also included a pledge from Faisal to support and help implement "large-scale" immigration of the Jews to Palestine. The terminology used in the agreement reveals a common understanding about the territories involved. Its use of the phrasing "Arab State and Palestine" indicates that, in the minds of the Arab and Zionist leaders in 1919, Palestine was not to be incorporated into the prospective Arab state. The two were envisioned as separate entities.

KEY TENETS OF THE FAISAL–WEIZMANN AGREEMENT

The Preamble to the Agreement states that the parties are "mindful of the racial kinship and ancient bonds existing between the Arabs and the Jewish people, and realiz[e] that the surest means of working out the consummation of their national aspirations, is through the closest possible collaboration in the development of the Arab State and Palestine."

Article I stipulated that "the Arab State and Palestine in all their relations and undertakings shall be controlled by the most cordial goodwill and understanding."

Article III referred to the future condition of Palestine, which "shall afford the fullest guarantees for carrying into effect the British Government's Declaration of the 2nd of November 1917 [i.e., the Balfour Declaration]."

In Article IV, recognition was given to the Jewish right to "large-scale" immigration into Palestine.

Articles IV and V contained provisions protecting the rights of the Arab tenant farmers and keeping Muslim Holy Places under the custody of Muslims.

The Faisal–Weizmann Agreement recognized the racial kinship and ancient bonds existing between the Arabs and the Jewish people. According to biblical sources, Abraham's son Isaac was the ancestor of the Jews, and Abraham's other son Ishmael was the ancestor of the Arab people.

The Signing of Peace in the Hall of Mirrors, Versailles 1919.

THE PARIS PEACE CONFERENCE

Just days after Faisal and Weizmann signed their agreement, the Paris Peace Conference began. Paris became the world's government, and the Supreme Council of the Principal Allied Powers its court of appeal and its parliament. The Supreme Council was authorized to establish new borders, and their decisions were recognized as law. These decisions changed the maps of Europe and the Middle East forever.

The Paris Peace Conference also saw the creation of a new international order—the League of Nations. The newly created League drew up a charter, called the Covenant of the League of Nations. It was made up of 26 articles. Article 22 of the Charter expressed a key principle. It stated that the well-being and development of specific peoples "not yet able to stand by themselves" ought to become "a sacred trust of civilization." This principle was especially relevant to the former Ottoman territories in the Middle East.

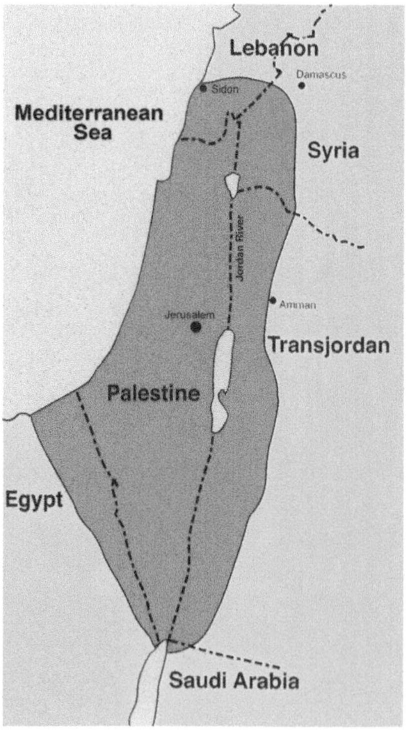

Map showing the boundaries of Palestine proposed by Zionists at the Paris Peace Conference, superimposed on modern boundaries.

- Arab States
- Area claimed by the World Zionist Organization at Paris Peace Conference
- – – – Current borders of Israel

Map labels: Lebanon, Damascus, Sidon, Mediterranean Sea, Syria, Jordan River, Jerusalem, Amman, Transjordan, Palestine, Egypt, Saudi Arabia

THE MANDATE SYSTEM

The provisions in Article 22 became the basis of the mandate system. This system assigned to advanced nations such as Great Britain and France the responsibility of guiding peoples "not yet able to stand by themselves." These advanced nations—known as Mandatories—would continue to meet these responsibilities until the fledgling states were ready for self-government.

Three weeks after the Arab petition at the Paris Conference, representatives of the Zionist Organization appeared before the Supreme Council. The plan they presented set out boundaries for the proposed Jewish State. The plan was based on the notion that the territory of the ancient Israelites was the historic home of the Jews, and should constitute their modern-day state.

The Jewish state was to include land west and east of the Jordan River. Faisal and the Arab delegation knew of the Zionist territorial requests and supported them. This is documented in a letter Faisal sent to Felix Frankfurter, an American delegate at the conference and a former U.S. Supreme Court Justice.

The Peace Conference produced peace treaties between the Allied Powers and Germany, Hungary, Austria, and Belgium. But it did not produce a peace treaty with Turkey. Nor did it resolve either of the following two questions: Which countries would be Mandatories for the former Turkish territories of Palestine, Syria, and Iraq? What would the borders of these territories be?

FAISAL'S LETTER TO FELIX FRANKFURTER

I wanted to take this opportunity ... to tell you what I have often been able to say to Dr. Weizmann in Akaba and in Europe. We feel that the Arabs and Jews are cousins in race, suffering similar oppressions ... and by a happy coincidence have been able to take the first steps toward the attainment of their national ideals together. We Arabs, especially the educated among us, look with deepest sympathy on the Zionist movement. Our deputation here in Paris is fully acquainted with the proposals submitted by the Zionist Organization to the Peace Conference, and we regard them as moderate and proper. We will do our best, in so far as we are concerned, to help them through; we will wish the Jews a most hearty welcome home.

We are working together for a reformed and revived Near East, and our two movements complete one another. The Jewish movement is national and not imperialistic. Our movement is national and not imperialistic and there is room in [Greater] Syria for us both.

I think that neither can be a real success without the other. People less informed and less responsible than our leaders, ignoring the need for co-operation of the Arabs and the Zionists, have been trying to exploit the local differences that must necessarily arise in Palestine in the early stages of our movements. Some of them have, I am afraid, misrepresented your aims to the Arab peasantry, with the result that interested parties have been able to make capital out of what they call differences. I wish to give you my firm conviction that these differences are not on question of principle, but on matters of detail, such as must inevitably occur in every contact with neighbouring peoples, and as are easily dissipated by mutual good will. ... I look forward, and my people with me look forward, to a future in which we will help you and you will help us, so that countries in which we are mutually interested may once again take their place in the community of civilized peoples of the world.

THE SAN REMO CONFERENCE

The next round of meetings concerning the former Ottoman territories took place in 1920, in the Italian resort city of San Remo. The Allied Powers convened there to establish the map of the "new" Middle East. Significant decisions were made. From the San Remo meetings emerged Mandates for Syria, Mesopotamia, and Palestine.

GREAT BRITAIN'S MAIN RESPONSIBILITY IN PALESTINE WAS TO FOLLOW THROUGH ON THE BALFOUR DECLARATION'S PLEDGES REGARDING THE NATIONAL HOME FOR THE JEWISH PEOPLE.

San Remo is very important in regards to Israel-Palestine. It established that the Balfour Declaration would be incorporated into the Mandate for Palestine. By incorporating the Declaration, the Mandate for Palestine became a special case, fundamentally different from the Mandates for Syria/Lebanon and Mesopotamia. Understanding this difference is a key to understanding the Zionist claim to Israel-Palestine.

The Mandates for Syria/Lebanon and Mesopotamia were focused on the actual communities living in those regions: the current inhabitants. In other words, the Mandatories of these regions were bound to consider—to accept as a "sacred trust"—the rights, interests, and wishes of the Arab populations currently living there.

World leaders in front of Villa Devachan in San Remo, Italy, where the conference took place. The San Remo conference established that the Balfour Declaration would be incorporated into the Mandate for Palestine.

The Mandate for Palestine, based on the Balfour Declaration, would not do this. In Palestine, the Mandatory (Great Britain) would not be responsible for assisting the predominant population (that is, the Arabs) to achieve self-determination. Instead, Great Britain's main responsibility in Palestine was to follow through on the Balfour Declaration's pledges regarding the national home for the Jewish people.

In other words, the San Remo Resolution fused two important ideas: the pledge of the 1917 Balfour Declaration, and the principles of Article 22 of the Covenant of the League of Nations. In doing so, it accomplished three things. First, it officially identified Palestine as the place where a Jewish national home would be established. Second, it reserved this Jewish national home not just for the 60,000 Jews living in Palestine at the end of World War I, but for the Jewish people as a whole—that is, for the approximately 15 million Jewish people worldwide. Palestine, as a leading British statesman said at San Remo, "was in the future to be the National Home of the Jews throughout the world." Third, it made the Jewish people worldwide the beneficiary of the principle of self-determination: one of the principles of Article 22 was that the developing nations being helped by the Mandatories were entitled to future self-government and independence. In the case of Palestine, this entitlement went not to the current Arab majority but to the existing and prospective Jewish inhabitants.

Preamble: Whereas the Principal Allied Powers have agreed that the Mandatory should be responsible for putting into effect the declaration [the Balfour Declaration] originally made on November 2nd, 1917, by the Government of His Britannic Majesty, and adopted by the said Powers, in favor of the establishment in Palestine of a national home for the Jewish people, it being clearly understood that nothing should be done which might prejudice the civil and religious rights of existing non-Jewish communities in Palestine, or the rights and political status enjoyed by Jews in any other country; recognition has thereby been given to the historical connection of the Jewish people with Palestine and to the grounds for reconstituting their national home in that country; and

Article II: The Mandatory shall be responsible for placing the country under such political, administrative and economic conditions as will secure the establishment of the Jewish national home, as laid down in the preamble, and the development of self-governing institutions, and also for safeguarding the civil and religious rights of all the inhabitants of Palestine, irrespective of race and religion. ...

Article IV: An appropriate Jewish agency shall be recognised as a public body for the purpose of advising and co-operating with the Administration of Palestine in such economic, social and other matters as may affect the establishment of the Jewish national home and the interests of the Jewish population in Palestine, and, subject always to the control of the Administration to assist and take part in the development of the country.

Article V: The Mandatory shall be responsible for seeing that no Palestine territory shall be ceded or leased to, or in any way placed under the control of the Government of any foreign Power.

Article VI: The Administration of Palestine, while ensuring that the rights and position of other sections of the population are not prejudiced, shall facilitate Jewish immigration under suitable conditions and shall encourage, in co-operation with the Jewish agency referred to in Article 4, close settlement by Jews on the land, including State lands and waste lands not required for public purposes. In Article IV, recognition was given to the Jewish right to "large-scale" immigration into Palestine.

Articles IV and V contained provisions protecting the rights of the Arab tenant farmers and keeping Muslim Holy Places under the custody of Muslims.

The Mandate document provided that Arabs living in Palestine would receive civil and religious rights, but not sovereignty rights. This was in keeping with Faisal's formal ceding of Palestine to Weizmann and the Zionists prior to and during the Paris Peace Conference. But the San Remo decisions also benefted the Arab people tremendously in terms of their territorial goals. The Allied Powers created mandates for Syria and Mesopotamia (Iraq)—that is, for most of the Middle East. With these mandates in place, tens of millions of Arabs received sovereignty rights in those regions, ending 500 years of Turkish rule. The San Remo decisions were ratified by the 51 members of the League of Nations in 1922, making them binding in international law.

THE MANDATE FOR PALESTINE, ARTICLE 22, AND THE PRINCIPLE OF SELF-DETERMINATION

When it came to the Mandate for Palestine, the Allied Powers chose to make the Jewish people worldwide, not the Arabs in Palestine, the beneficiaries of the "sacred trust" described in Article 22. This meant that the right to self-determination in Palestine went to the Jewish people, not to the Arab majority there.

The Arabs believe this decision was unjust. Their reasoning is simple: at the beginning of the 20th century, they themselves were the majority population in the region and had been since the 13th century CE. Their view is that Wilson's principle of self-determination should have applied to them, and they should not have been disposed of—"dominated and governed"—except by their own consent.

The Jewish people point to other considerations. They point to the fact that Palestine was their ancient homeland and that Palestine had been Turkish territory, not Arab territory, since 1517. The Supreme Council of the Allied Powers and the 51 member states of League of Nations gave to the Arab peoples all of the Turks' former territory in the Middle East except for the very small portion reserved for the Jewish people. A commission headed by Woodrow Wilson—who introduced the concept of self-determination and was himself fully in favour of a Jewish state in Palestine—explained as follows the Allied Powers' support for the Zionist plan:

It was the cradle and home of their vital race, which has made large spiritual contributions to mankind, and is the only land in which they can hope to find a home of their own, they being in this last respect, unique among significant peoples.

When Faisal appeared before the Supreme Council on February 6th, he specifically excluded Palestine from the territory he asked for. This exclusion was consistent with the Faisal–Weizmann Agreement he had made only weeks before.

Palestine was always a special case within the mandate system—a prospective state not for the Arab majority living there in 1919, who at the time numbered approximately 600,000, but for the Jewish people throughout the world, who numbered 15 million. By the unique terms of the Mandate for Palestine, in other words, the Jewish people were the majority population in Palestine and warranted the right to self-determination.

Woodrow Wilson of the United States (right) was fully in favour of a Jewish state in Palestine. He and (left to right) David Lloyd George of Britain, Vittorio Orlando of Italy, and Georges Clemenceau of France formed the Council of Four—the top Allied leaders who met at the Paris Peace Conference.

ISRAEL-PALESTINE UNDER THE BRITISH MANDATE: 1920–1947

Jews evacuate the Old City of Jerusalem after Arab riots in 1936, ecorted by British soldiers.

Even though the San Remo Conference greatly benefited the Arab people overall, the Arabs living in Palestine—1 percent of the total Arab population—were not content with the outcome. In the wake of the San Remo decisions, Arab leaders in Palestine stirred up opposition and hostility to the British and Zionist efforts.

There followed violent Arab uprisings against Jewish communities in Palestine, with deaths and casualties on both sides. In May of 1921, the British appointed a commission of inquiry to investigate the cause of the violence. The report produced by the com-

mission marked a significant change in the British government's attitude toward its responsibilities as Mandatory in Palestine. As the British sought to contain and resolve the Arab-Jewish conflict, their policies began to diverge from the aims of the Mandate and their obligations under it.

The British government's solution to Arab violence was to partition mandate Palestine and create a prospective new Arab state east of the Jordan River, called Transjordan. In other words, there was now a prospective Arab state in "east" Palestine and a prospective Jewish state in "west" Palestine. The new British protectorate of Transjordan consisted of 77 percent of the territory originally earmarked for Mandatory Palestine.

Al-Hajj Muhammad on horseback (left front) with his followers. Abd al-Rahim al-Hajj Muhammad was a prominent Palestinian Arab commander of rebel forces during the 1936–39 Arab revolt against the British Mandate.

THE YISHUV AND THE ARAB NATIONALISTS

On the ground in Israel, the actual building of the Jewish National home was being done by the early settlers of the *Yishuv*. This was the Jewish community that had begun forming in Palestine in the late 19th century. Many of them were refugees from Eastern Europe, carried to Israel by Zionist ideals. By the 1920s and 1930s, the leaders of the *Yishuv* were seeing that political Zionism—the Jewish nationalistic endeavor—was on a collision course with Arab nationalism in Palestine.

This inevitable clash became clear to David Ben Gurion, an important early leader of the Yishuv (and, later, Israel's first prime minister), during his 1936 meetings with George Antonius, a leading Arab figure. After his talks with Antonius in May 1936, Ben Gurion stated publicly for the first time that there was a conflict between Arab and Jewish nationalism in Palestine. "We and they want the same thing: We both want Palestine. And that is the fundamental conflict."

The term Yishuv refers to the body of Jewish residents that arrived and lived in Palestine before the establishment of the State of Israel.

The British policy of trying to appease the Palestinian Arab leadership with concessions, usually made at the expense of their earlier pledges to the Jewish people, became a pattern during the mandate years. The Arabs fell into a pattern, too; British concessions only deepened their intransigence. For example, when the British tried to establish a joint Arab–Jewish representative body to advise them, the Arab Executive not only rejected the proposal; they made further demands for quotas on Jewish immigration and land sales to Jews. (Ironically, it was the wealthy Arab landowning elites who were selling huge parcels of land in Palestine to Jewish buyers, at significantly inflated prices, and thereby divesting poor Arab tenant farmers of their livelihood.)

ISRAEL-PALESTINE IN THE NEW MIDDLE EAST

FATHER OF PALESTINIAN NATIONALISM: HAJ AMIN AL-HUSSEINI

Born into an elite land-owning family in the region of Jerusalem, Haj Amin al Husseini (1897–1974) led the Palestinian Arabs for the better part of three decades. He exerted a tremendous influence on the Arab population of Palestine during the 1920s and 1930s. This influence has done much to damage Arab–Jewish relations in the region to the present day.

As the Grand Mufti of Jerusalem, Husseini incited anti-Jewish riots in the Old City in the 1920s, during which Jewish women and children were massacred. He headed the Nazi's Arab Office in Berlin under Hitler in the 1930s (the two men agreed on the best solution to the "Jewish problem" in their respective regions). And, during World War II, he organized a Muslim SS Division in Yugoslavia that committed many atrocities including the slaughter of 200,000 Orthodox Christian Serbs for which he was subsequently indicted for war crimes. Husseini was also a co-founder of the Arab League, in 1944. Later, during his exile in Egypt, he was a mentor to Yasser Arafat.

Haj Amin al-Husseini meeting with Adolf Hitler in December 1941. Husseini's anti-Semitic policies continue in the PA and Hamas today.

THE PEEL REPORT OF 1937 CONCLUDED THAT ARAB AND JEWISH INTERESTS IN PALESTINE COULD NOT BE RECONCILED AND THAT THE MANDATE WAS UNWORKABLE.

As Jewish institution-building grew, the most powerful Arab leader in Palestine, Haj Amin al Husseini—the Grand Mufti of Jerusalem—continued to incite the Arab community to violence. There were several significant episodes in the 1920s and 1930s, including the massacre of 66 Jews in Hebron in August of 1929. Another wave of violence began in April of 1936, when

Husseini mobilized an Arab protest against the British. He called on Arabs to join a national strike and stop paying taxes to the British mandatory government until it had put an end to Jewish immigration and to land sales to Jews, and had established an Arab government. All three demands directly contravened the provisions of the Mandate for Palestine.

The British finally ordered the deportation of Husseini, removing the uprising's immediate cause. By this time, however, the Arab revolt had had disastrous results. Thousands of Arabs had been killed or wounded by the British, and the Arab economy in Palestine was crippled.

Following the revolt, the British government established another commission of inquiry. The resulting report—the Peel Report of 1937—concluded that Arab and Jewish interests in Palestine could not be reconciled and that the Mandate was unworkable. The report recommended that Jewish immigration be limited, that Arab sales of land to Jews be restricted, and that an Arab agency be created, modeled on the Jewish Agency—in other words, a public body for the purpose of advising and cooperating with the administration of Palestine. The report's conclusions went even further, stating that the Mandate should be terminated and that Palestine—what was left of it after the 1921 creation of Transjordan—be further partitioned into independent Arab and Jewish states.

Map of the amendment to the original Palestine Mandate boundaries

▨ Arab States
Syria and Lebanon (French Mandate)
Iraq and Transjordan (British Mandate)

▨ Proposed Jewish State
(British Mandate)

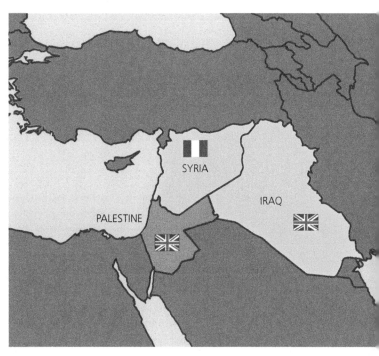

Map of the original Palestine Mandate boundaries.

▨ Arab States
Syria and Lebanon (French Mandate)
Iraq (British Mandate)

▨ Proposed Jewish State
(British Mandate)

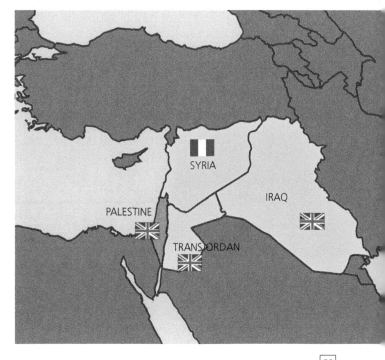

ISRAEL-PALESTINE IN THE NEW MIDDLE EAST

According to this new partition plan, the new Arab state would receive 80 percent of the territory west of the Jordan River and would be united with Jordan. The Jewish state would be given 20 percent of the land west of the Jordan River. In other words, this second two-state solution gave the Jews approximately 10 percent of the land originally allocated for the Jewish national home. The Jewish leadership, wanting an end to the Arab violence, was prepared to accept the new partition plan. But the Arab leadership rejected it, and it never came to fruition.

Jewish demonstration against the White Paper in Jerusalem in 1939.

By May 1939, Britain was facing war with Germany and wanted to reduce its commitments abroad. The British government drafted yet another white paper. This time it was the MacDonald White Paper, which proposed that Palestine become a unitary state—in other words, no longer a Jewish state but an independent Arab state, with a two-thirds Arab majority and a Jewish population not exceeding one-third of the total. The white paper put a five-year limit on Jewish immigration. At the end of that time, no Jews would be allowed to immigrate to Palestine without the consent of the Arabs.

This was a drastic revision of the original goal of a "national home for the Jewish people" in Palestine. It also showed the British government betraying its legal responsibilities as Mandatory in Palestine. The Zionist Organization declared the MacDonald White Paper unacceptable, as did the League of Nations' Mandate Commission. So did the Arab leadership—to the dismay and astonishment of the British.

The timing of the 1939 White Paper was tragic for European Jewry. In January 1939, Nazi Germany was already moving toward its "Final Solution." Over the next five years, the Jews of Europe underwent mass extermination. The British authorities, despite

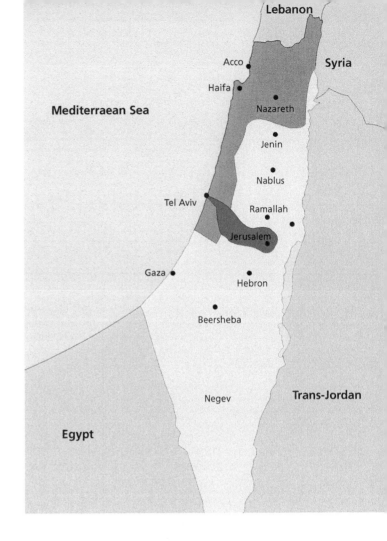

the League of Nations' rejection of the White Paper, continued to deny entry to Jewish refugees seeking asylum in Palestine. While 6 million Jews perished in the concentration camps, the British enforced the White Paper's policies.

After World War II, the British continued restricting Jewish immigration to Palestine even though hundreds of thousands of Jews, survivors of the Holocaust, remained in displaced persons camps. The British remained deaf to pleas from the Jewish leadership and even from the international community. The Zionists became outraged. Attacks on British property followed, and violence escalated between Jews and Arabs. On July 22, 1946, a Jewish paramilitary group blew up the King David Hotel in Jerusalem, killing over 80 people, mostly British military personnel.

The growing chaos led the British government to announce, in 1947, that it would ask the United Nations to make recommendations regarding a solution for Palestine.

WHILE 6 MILLION JEWS PERISHED IN THE CONCENTRATION CAMPS, THE BRITISH ENFORCED THE WHITE PAPER'S POLICIES.

The British in 1947, overwhelmed by the problems in Palestine, handed off their Mandate obligations to the fledgling United Nations (UN). The UN appointed a Special Committee on Palestine (UNSCOP) to make recommendations on the future of the territory. The result was another two-state solution.

The committee recommended that nearly half of what remained of Mandate Palestine—that is, half of the territory west of the Jordan—be allotted to the Arabs. According to the plan, the population of the Jewish state was to be 45 percent Arab, while the new Arab state would be 1 percent Jewish.

Map of thge Peel Partition Plan for Palestine. (1937)

Proposed Arab State

Proposed Jewish State

Proposed International Zone

THE UNITED NATIONS AND THE PARTITION OF PALESTINE

The UN General Assembly received the UNSCOP recommendations and approved Resolution 181 (the "Partition Resolution") on November 29, 1947. Thirty-three nations voted in favor of it. Since Resolution 181 was a General Assembly motion (rather than a Security Council decision), it was not binding in international law; it could become a legal agreement only if both Jewish and Arab representatives accepted it.

The Jewish leadership had compelling reasons to reject the Partition Resolution. From their point of view, it would have meant the second time in 30 years that Palestine had been partitioned to the significant territorial advantage of the Palestinian Arabs. The national home for the Jewish people under the British Mandate, as set out at San Remo, was to include territory on both the east and west sides of the Jordan River. If we take into account the previous partition of Palestine—the one that, in 1921, created Transjordan in the territory east of the Jordan river—this new plan meant that the Jewish state was to be established in a territory approximately one-eighth the size of the territory originally allotted for it.

But the Jewish leadership accepted the resolution. Pressure on them to do so came from several sources. Not the least consideration was the fact that hundreds of thousands of European Jews, displaced by World War II, were living in refugee camps with nowhere to go.

Table showing Arab and Jewish demographics under the Partition Plan.

Territory Allocation	Arab and Other Population	% Arab and Other	Jewish Population	% Jewish	Total Population
Arab State	725,000	99%	10,000	1%	735,000
Jewish State	407,000	45%	498,000	55%	905,000
International*	105,000	51%	100,000	49%	205,000
Total	1,237,000	67%	608,000	33%	1,845,000

Source: UNSCOP Report 1947

*The U.N. plan called for an expansion of the municipal boundaries of Jerusalem to create an Arab majority in the International Zone.

Map of United Nations Partition Plan for Palestine, adopted on November 29th 1947.

Proposed Arab State

Proposed Jewish State

Jerusalem (International Zone)

Jewish reservations about the new partition plan proved irrelevant. The Arab leadership flatly rejected it. And they made it clear that any attempt to implement it would lead to war. Why did the Arab leaders reject the 1947 partition plan? They thought it unfair that it gave 57 percent of the land to 37 percent of the people. Their view was that the Jews ought to be a minority population in a unitary Palestinian state.

Did the Arabs have a point? After all, the Jews constituted only about 30 percent of Palestine's population in 1947. Arab objections need to be considered in the context of all of the regional mandates and their allocations. The Mandates for Syria and Iraq gave political rights to the tens of millions of Arab people living in the remaining regions of the Middle East—millions of square miles of land that, until that point and for hundreds of years previously, had been sovereign Turkish territory.

By contrast, the Allied Powers reserved an area of approximately ten thousand square miles for the 15 million Jewish people around the world who would be prospective citizens of the Jewish state.

THE JEWISH LEADERSHIP ACCEPTED THE RESOLUTION. THE ARAB LEADERSHIP FLATLY REJECTED IT. AND THEY MADE IT CLEAR THAT ANY ATTEMPT TO IMPLEMENT IT WOULD LEAD TO WAR.

THE 1948 WAR
AND ITS LEGACIES

The British completed the withdrawal of their armed forces on May 14, 1948, and Israel declared independence the same day. The next day, Arab armies from Transjordan, Syria, Lebanon, Iraq, and Egypt attacked Israel.

The Arab League explained the invasion to the UN as a necessity, a means of establishing security and order. The UN rejected this rationale for military force.

The war continued through 1948 and into the next year. In early 1949, after UN-mediated discussions, Israel signed an armistice agreement with Jordan.

TERRITORIAL EFFECTS: THE WEST BANK

The 1949 Armistice Line—the Green Line—has become one of the most significant dividing lines in Middle East history. It demarcates the territory now called the West Bank, so named because it's on the west bank of the Jordan River. Prior to the 1948 war, there was no distinct territory called the West Bank. The territory took on that name only after Jordan occupied it in the wake of the 1948 War. Before that, it was called Judea

Territory held on June 1, 1948 after the initial Arab Invasion.

- Territory held by Arabs
- Territory held by Israel

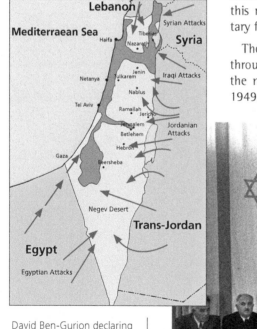

David Ben-Gurion declaring independence of Israel on May 14, 1948.

and Samaria and was considered part of the national home for the Jewish people under the Palestine Mandate.

According to the provisions of the 1949 Armistice Agreement, the Green Line did not constitute a border and was not supposed to be used to determine territorial rights. Nonetheless, the UN continually evokes it in its efforts to broker peace between Israel and the Palestinian Authority. Almost every Arab–Israeli peace plan has earmarked the West Bank as the territory of the future Palestinian state.

Israeli policemen meet a Jordanian legionnaire near the Mandelbaum Gate on the Green Line that divided Jerusalem between 1949 and 1967.

REFUGEES

Another legacy of the 1948 war was refugees. As a result of the war, hundreds of thousands of Arabs who lived west of the Jordan River were displaced. The Palestine Arabs referred to their displacement as the *Nakba*—the catastrophe. The Palestinian Authority hold Israel responsible. They are supported in this by the UN and by many members of the international community. Some have alleged that Israel engaged in the "ethnic cleansing" of Judea and Samaria (the West Bank) during the war. Supporters of the Palestinian Authority maintain, further, that Israel should allow the refugees from the 1948 war to return to their original homes or should compensate them and their descendants for the loss of their property and livelihoods.

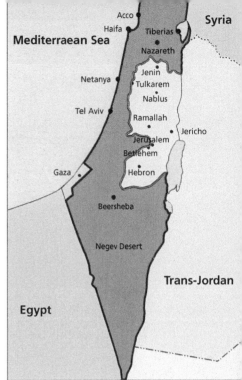

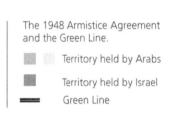

The 1948 Armistice Agreement and the Green Line.

- Territory held by Arabs
- Territory held by Israel
- Green Line

LOCATION OF THE HOLY SITES

If the Green Line were to become the border between Israel and a future Palestinian state, the following holy sites would no longer be located within the State of Israel: the Temple Mount in the Old City, which is Judaism's holiest site and the ultimate bone of contention in the Arab–Israeli conflict; and the Church of the Holy Sepulchre, which covers the ground on which Jesus was crucified and buried.

Does it matter who controls these Jewish and Christian holy sites? History shows that the religious rights and holy sites of all faiths in the Old City have fared best under Israeli control. Between 1948 and 1967, when the Jordanians governed the Old City, synagogues were destroyed, cemeteries desecrated, and Jews prohibited from entering the Old City or from worshipping at the Western Wall. Jews were not given access to the sacred Jewish burial grounds on the Mount of Olives. The Jordanians also prevented Christians from visiting their holy places except for special ceremonial events, such as Christmas. This contravened the 1949 Armistice Agreement. Since 1967, the freedom of worship and the holy sites of all faiths have been respected.

THE DISPLACEMENT OF PALESTINIAN ARABS

Why did so many Arabs leave in 1948? The traditional Arab narrative is that they were forcibly expelled by Israeli soldiers and paramilitaries. The traditional Zionist narrative is that they were instructed to leave by their own Arab leaders.

Extensive research carried out since the war, based on archival documents and testimonials from both sides, has revealed a much more nuanced picture.

To be sure, a small number of Arabs in Palestine were forcibly expelled. And a small number were instructed to leave by their own leaders. But the vast majority of Arabs left their homes by choice. Why? They left their homes for the reason that any civilian population flees a war zone: from fear of being caught up in battle, fear of being hurt or killed. They wanted to get clear of the fighting.

But what about the Arabs who were forcibly expelled?

In considering this question, it's important to keep in mind two things: the political context of the 1948 war; and the nature of war itself. Let's start with the political context. Just prior to the war, the Jews had accepted the UN partition resolution; the Arab leadership had rejected it. In other words, the representatives of the Arab people living in Palestine had rejected a peaceful proposal to divide the country into two states, one Arab and one Jewish. When the Arab leaders rejected the offer and went to war against Israel, the Jewish side was forced to try to secure themselves and their territory. The Palestinian National Movement, led by Haj Amin al-Husseini, had made it clear that the Arab intention was the total destruction of the Jewish people in the region—another Holocaust. This intention was publicly expressed by Husseini and by Arab leaders from other countries.

Jaramana Refugee Camp in Damascus, Syria. During the 1948 Palestine War, around 85% of the Palestinian Arab population of what has become Israel left their homes. They fled to the West Bank and Gaza, and to the countries of Lebanon, Syria and Jordan

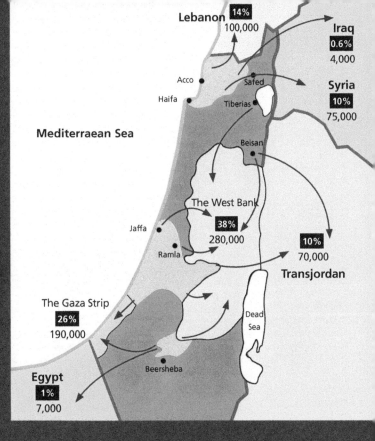

Now let's consider the nature of war itself. Wars are chaotic events in which terrible things happen inevitably. This was true of the 1948 war as of every war ever fought. As one noted historian has said, "[E]very war has its dark side, especially civil wars, which are notably vicious. And '48 also had a dark side, which involved the displacement of 700,000 people." The Israelis did not seek the 1948 war. On one side was the Arab intention to expel the Jewish community from Palestine. On the other side was the Jewish intention to defend itself against such expulsion. The Jewish effort involved, in some cases, the displacement of Palestinian Arabs, removed by Jewish military forces not for the purpose of "ethnic cleansing" but for strategic purposes. Their primary aim was security.

Distribution of Arab refugees after the 1948 War. The United Nations estimated that over 725,00 Arabs fled between April and December 1948.

- Main areas from which Arabs fled
- Percentage of refugees reaching new areas
- Towns with large Arab population, most of whom fled
- 000 UN estimate of the number of refugees reaching new areas

Palestine refugees making their way from Galilee in October–November 1948.

JEWISH REFUGEES

The 1948 war also created a Jewish refugee problem. After the war, Jewish people living in Arab countries suffered a backlash. This happened in Iraq, for example, where Jewish communities had existed for 2,500 years. (They had been there since the first diaspora, which followed the Babylonian conquest of Judea.) Hundreds of Jews in that country were murdered, thousands imprisoned, and Jewish synagogues, shops, and homes were burned and destroyed. This pattern was repeated in other Arab countries. Between 1948 and the mid-70s, over 800,000 Jews were stripped of all they owned and driven out.

A Yemenite family walking through the desert to a camp near the seaport city of Aden in Yemen. 49,000 Yemenite Jews were airlifted (inset) to safety in the new state of Israel between June 1949 and September 1950 during an operation called Operation Magic Carpet.

Jewish refugees at Ma'abarot transit camp. The Ma'abarot were refugee absorption camps in Israel in the 1950s. The camps were meant to provide accommodation for the large influx of Jewish refugees and new Jewish immigrants arriving in the newly independent State of Israel.

The UN has passed a number of resolutions concerning the rights of Arab refugees and runs an entire organization specifically for Palestine Arabs called UNWRA. But no UN resolutions have been passed concerning Jewish refugees—the civilian populations expelled from Arab countries. (In November 2013, the government of Canada published a report titled "Recognizing Jewish Refugees from the Middle East and North Africa").

The majority of Jewish refugees were absorbed by the fledgling Jewish State. Tragically, many Arab refugees from 1948 were not offered the same opportunities by the Arab states in the region. They remain stateless to this day.

THE MAJORITY OF JEWISH REFUGEES WERE ABSORBED BY THE FLEDGLING JEWISH STATE. TRAGICALLY, MANY ARAB REFUGEES FROM 1948 WERE NOT OFFERED THE SAME OPPORTUNITIES BY THE ARAB STATES IN THE REGION. THEY REMAIN STATELESS TO THIS DAY.

Jewish refugees who went to Israel from Arab lands between May 1948 and May 1972.

Arab Middle East   Israel-Palestine   Arab countries

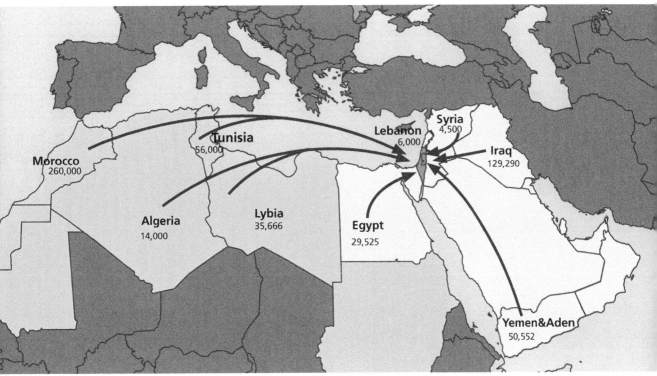

Morocco
260,000

Tunisia
56,000

Algeria
14,000

Lybia
35,666

Egypt
29,525

Lebanon
6,000

Syria
4,500

Iraq
129,290

Yemen&Aden
50,552

1967: SIX-DAY WAR

King Hussein of Jordan (left), President Gamal Abdel Nasser of Egypt and Egyptian Army Chief of Staff Abdel Hakim Amer in the headquarters of the Supreme Command of the Armed Forces in Cairo before signing Egyptian-Jordanian-Iraqi defense pact prior to the Six-Day War.

Twenty years after Israel's War of Independence, the country found itself again at war with the Arab states. This war was over in six days. Israel prevailed swiftly following a preemptive strike against Egypt, the main aggressor.

LEADUP TO THE '67 WAR

Despite the treaties and agreements of 1949, the Arab states viewed Israel as an illegitimate state and waited for their opportunity to attack again. By the late 1960s, Arab rulers believed they had gained the military advantage over their enemy. Under the leadership of President Nasser of Egypt, they directed a series of clear provocations at Israel.

In mid-May 1967, Nasser moved two divisions of his armed forces into the Sinai Peninsula. The next day, he ordered the United Nations Emergency Force (UNEF), a peace-keeping force positioned in the Sinai, to relocate to camps in the Gaza Strip. Egypt had no authority over UNEF, but UNEF acceded to Nasser's demands.

The following week, Nasser announced a blockade against Israeli ships in the Strait of Tiran, cutting off access to and from the port city of Eilat in the south of Israel. The official declaration targeted Israel: "The Strait of Tiran is part of our territorial waters. No Israeli ship will ever navi-

Chief of Staff Lt. Gen. Yitzhak Rabin (front left) led the Israeli armed forces during the Six-Day War.

gate it again. We also forbid the shipment of strategic materials to Israel on non-Israeli vessels."

Israel appealed to the UN to break the blockade and pointed out that, under Article 51 of the UN Charter, it had the right to defend itself against an act of aggression. The UN offered no solution. Nasser, noting the sluggish international reaction, decided Israel was isolated and vulnerable.

Three days later, on May 25, the governments of Syria, Iraq, Jordan, and Saudi Arabia, following Egypt's directives, began mobilizing troops along Israel's borders. By May 31, Egypt had moved 100,000 troops, 1,000 tanks, and 500 heavy guns into the Sinai buffer zone—the area between Israel and Egypt that had been established as neutral under earlier armistice agreements.

Israel's many appeals to the UN failed to prevent a conflict. On Sunday, June 4, Israeli Prime Minister Levi Eshkol convened an emergency War Cabinet meeting and passed a resolution to launch a preemptive strike against the Arab States, now clearly poised for war. The Jewish state's 264,000 soldiers, 800 tanks, and 300 combat aircraft would attempt to defend Israel against the combined strength of the Arabs' 350,000 soldiers, 2,000 tanks, and 700 aircraft.

ARAB RHETORIC IN THE LEADUP TO THE 1967 WAR

Just before the war began, outbursts of anti-Israel statements came from Arab leaders and from the Arab states' government-controlled radios. On May 27, just a few days before the war, Nasser summed up the Arab objectives: "Our basic objective will be the destruction of Israel. The Arab people want to fight. ... The mining of Sharm el Sheikh [the Strait of Tiran] is a confrontation with Israel. Adopting this measure obligates us to be ready to embark on a general war with Israel."

Nasser's statements were followed by those of Iraqi President Aref, on May 31: "The existence of Israel is an error which must be rectified. This is our opportunity to wipe out the ignominy which has been with us since 1948. Our goal is clear—to wipe Israel off the map."

A few days later, on June 1, the chairman of the Palestine Liberation Organization (PLO), Ahmed Shukairy, declared the following: "This is a fight for a homeland. It is either us or the Israelis. There is no middle road. The Jews of Palestine will have to leave. ... Any of the old Palestine Jewish population who survive may stay, but it is my impression that none of them will survive."

ISRAEL'S MANY APPEALS TO THE UN FAILED TO PREVENT A CONFLICT. ON SUNDAY, JUNE 4, ISRAELI PRIME MINISTER LEVI ESHKOL CONVENED AN EMERGENCY WAR CABINET MEETING AND PASSED A RESOLUTION TO LAUNCH A PREEMPTIVE STRIKE AGAINST THE ARAB STATES.

Israel's decisive victory in the Six-Day War included the capture of the Gaza Strip and the Sinai Peninsula from Egypt, the West Bank and East Jerusalem from Jordan, and the Golan Heights from Syria.

MAIN EVENTS OF THE WAR

On June 5, 1967, Israel launched an aerial attack that destroyed almost all of the Egyptian air force. The Israeli prime minister sent word to King Hussein of Jordan, through the UN and the Americans, that if Jordan stayed out of the war, Israel would not attack them. Had Jordan complied, its occupation of the West Bank and the Old City of Jerusalem would have continued as it had since 1948. That did not happen, however. Jordan's response was to shell Israel.

Chief of Staff Lt. Gen. Yitzhak Rabin (left) in the entrance to the old city of Jerusalem during the Six Day War, with Moshe Dayan (center) and Uzi Narkiss.

Once Jordan joined the war, the Israeli Cabinet gave the go-ahead to the Israel Defense Forces (IDF) to take the Old City of Jerusalem. When the Israelis entered the Old City in June 1967, they found that all but one of the 35 synagogues there had been destroyed. These synagogues were centuries old. In the ancient graveyard on the Mount of Olives, the Jordanians had defaced or profaned 38,000 of the 50,000 Jewish graves. Nonetheless, recapturing the Old City was a profoundly joyful event for the Jewish people. When Israeli soldiers prayed at the Western Wall on June 7, 1967, it marked the end of nearly 2,000 years of restricted Jewish access to their holiest site—the Temple Mount.

Shortly after capturing the Temple Mount/Haram al-Sharif in the Old City, the government of Israel made the decision to return custody of it to Muslim administrators. This was a remarkable decision, considering that Jewish access to the area had been denied under Jordanian occupation and that the Temple Mount is the holiest site in Judaism.

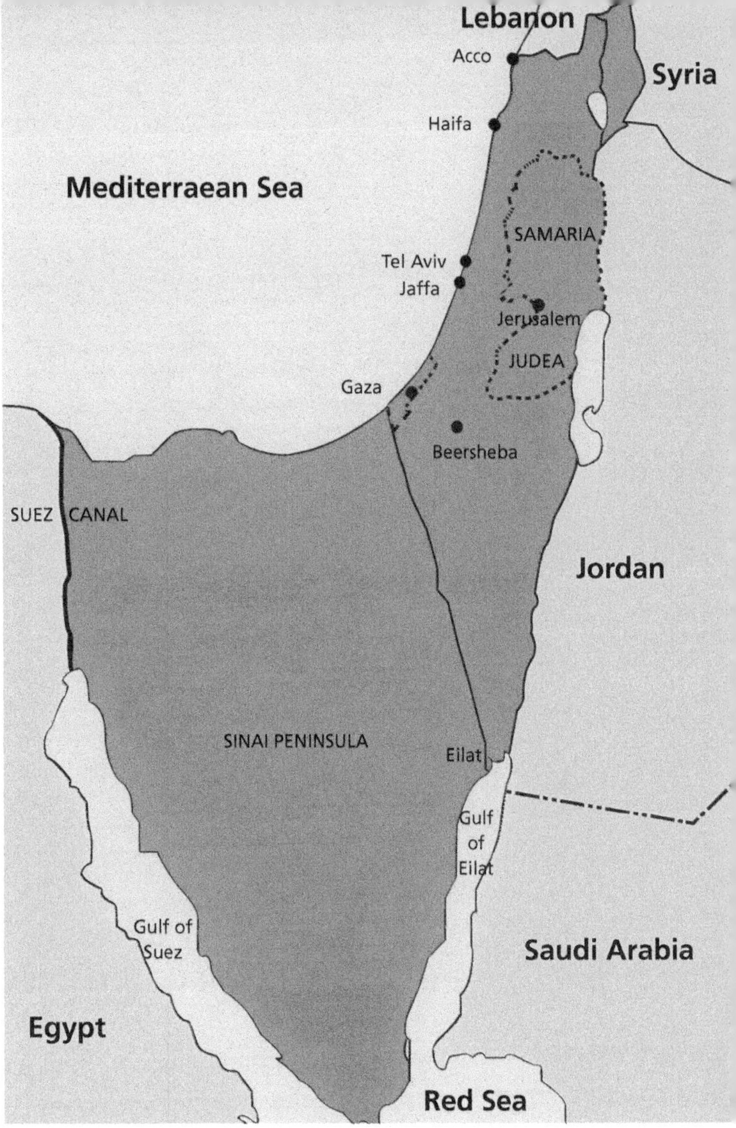

Map labels: Lebanon, Acco, Haifa, Syria, Mediterraean Sea, SAMARIA, Tel Aviv, Jaffa, Jerusalem, JUDEA, Gaza, Beersheba, Jordan, SUEZ CANAL, SINAI PENINSULA, Eilat, Gulf of Eilat, Gulf of Suez, Saudi Arabia, Egypt, Red Sea

At the end of the Six-Day War, Israel controlled the West Bank, the Gaza Strip, the Sinai Peninsula, and the Golan Heights. Before the war, all of these territories had been held by the defeated Arab nations.

POLITICAL AFTERMATH OF THE 1967 WAR

Two weeks after the war, the Israeli parliament—the Knesset—enacted legislation to include the Old City and east Jerusalem under Israeli administration and Israeli law. A week later, the UN General Assembly passed Resolution 2253, declaring Israel's measures invalid and calling upon the Israeli government to rescind them. Since then, the UN has opposed Israel's reunification of Jerusalem and its claims to sovereignty over it.

Israel's new legislation also included the Protection of Holy Places Law 5727 (1967). This Act stipulated that holy places were to be protected from desecration and "anything likely to violate the freedom of access of the members of the different religions to the places sacred to them or their feelings with regard to those places." Israel gave the Muslim Waqf—the governing body that oversees Muslim endowments—the authority to administer various Muslim holy sites, including the Temple Mount/Haram Al-Sharif, the Dome of the Rock, and the Al-Aqsa Mosque. Since 1967, Israel has continued to protect all faiths' freedom of access to their holy sites.

Territory held by Israel after the 1967 War.

■ Arab States

■ Israel's Territory

SINCE 1967, ISRAEL HAS CONTINUED TO PROTECT ALL FAITHS' FREEDOM OF ACCESS TO THEIR HOLY SITES.

1967: WAR OF SELF-DEFENCE OR WAR OF AGGRESSION?

Opinions differ as to whether Israel acted with aggression or in self-defense in the 1967 war. The UN General Assembly, so often opposed to Israeli policies, considered Israel's preemptive strike to be a legitimate response to the situation. The Arab states claim otherwise.

Israel's Position: A pre-emptive strike was necessary because of the following: (1) the Arabs' deploying hundreds of thousands of troops and thousands of tanks and heavy artillery on Israel's borders; (2) Egypt's blockading the straits of Tiran; and (3) announcements from the governments of Egypt and Iraq, as well as from the PLO Chairman, about a unified effort to destroy the State of Israel. After the unified Arab attack in 1948, Israel had every reason to suspect that an attack was imminent.

Arab Position: The Israeli claim that they were facing an existential threat was false. They made this claim in order to justify launching the pre-emptive attack that led to their capturing and occupying the rest of Palestine. Israel's attack on Egypt, which provoked the 1967 War, was just one more in a line of aggressive moves from Israel that threatened and undermined Arab rights in the region.

OPINIONS DIFFER AS TO WHETHER ISRAEL ACTED WITH AGGRESSION OR IN SELF-DEFENSE.

THE WEST BANK

The Six-Day War changed the dynamic of the Arab–Israeli relationship. This was especially true in areas previously under Jordanian control: the West Bank and Jerusalem. After June 1967, over 600,000 Arabs living in the West Bank (the disputed territories) were brought under Israeli military administration.

The UN, along with the world media and various human rights organizations—Amnesty International, for example—often portrays Israeli administration over the West Bank territories as very detrimental to the millions of Arabs living in the region. But, in the years immediately following the 1967 war, the Israelis encouraged and financed economic development in the West Bank. By the end of 1970, Arab unemployment there had dropped from 12 percent to 3 percent. By 1972, 600,000 Arabs from the West Bank found their daily employment in Israel, and 44,000 Arabs who had fled from the West Bank in 1967 had returned. These positive trends continued until the Yom Kippur War of 1973.

SECURITY COUNCIL RESOLUTION 242

On November 22, 1967, the Security Council of the UN passed Resolution 242. This resolution required Israel to withdraw from the West Bank, Gaza, the Sinai, and the Golan Heights on the condition that the Arabs recognize Israel's right to live in peace. The UN Resolution labeled the Israeli presence in the recently captured territories an "occupation."

Resolution 242 is one of the most important of the UN resolutions regarding the Arab–Israeli conflict. To this day, it is a cornerstone of diplomatic efforts in the Middle East. Not surprisingly, Israel and the Arabs have interpreted Resolution 242 differently.

RESOLUTION 242 IS ONE OF THE MOST IMPORTANT OF THE UN RESOLUTIONS REGARDING THE ARAB–ISRAELI CONFLICT. TO THIS DAY, IT IS A CORNERSTONE OF DIPLOMATIC EFFORTS IN THE MIDDLE EAST.

RESOLUTION 242

The Security Council,

Expressing its continuing concern with the grave situation in the Middle East,

Emphasizing the inadmissibility of the acquisition of territory by war and the need to work for a just and lasting peace in which every State in the area can live in security,

Emphasizing further that all Member States in their acceptance of the Charter of the United Nations have undertaken a commitment to act in accordance with Article 2 of the Charter,

1. *Affirms* that the fulfillment of Charter principles requires the establishment of a just and lasting peace in the Middle East which should include the application of both the following principles:

    (i) Withdrawal of Israeli armed forces from territories occupied in the recent conflict;

    (ii) Termination of all claims or states of belligerency and respect for and acknowledgement of the sovereignty, territorial integrity and political independence of every State in the area and their right to live in peace within secure and recognized boundaries free from threats or acts of force;

2. *Affirms further* the necessity

    (a) For guaranteeing freedom of navigation through international waterways in the area;

    (b) For achieving a just settlement of the refugee problem;

    (c) For guaranteeing the territorial inviolability and political independence of every State in the area, through measures including the establishment of demilitarized zones.

Israel has taken the resolution to mean that it did not have to withdraw from all the territories occupied and that withdrawal would only take place after the completion of a direct negotiation process between the parties involved. That negotiating process needed to include the determination of "secure and recognized boundaries" and the signing of a peace treaty. In other words, any settlement would have to involve official Arab recognition of the State of Israel. Such recognition—an acknowledgment of Israel's right to exist—has been a key requirement by Israel in every peace initiative to date.

The Arabs took Resolution 242 to mean that Israel had first to withdraw from all the territories occupied in 1967 before negotiations could begin. Many Arabs today argue that peace between the Arabs and Jews in the Middle East has always depended on the withdrawal of Israel from all the territories occupied in 1967. They blame Israel's refusal to withdraw for the fact that there is today no peace in the Middle East. Is this a valid argument? A number of jurists and many in the international community support the Arab position.

Others do not. Golda Meir pointed out that Arab possession of these territories had not prevented them from starting the Six-Day War. Why would the Arabs suddenly turn peaceable if these territories were returned to them? Her words were as follows:

> [I]n June 1967, the Sinai, the Gaza strip, the West Bank, the Golan Heights and East Jerusalem [including the Old City] all were in Arab possession, so that it is ludicrous to argue today that Israel's presence in those territories since 1967 is the cause of tension in the Middle East or was the cause of the Yom Kippur War [in 1973].

Golda Meir was Israel's
Prime Minister from
1969 to 1974.

WHAT IS "OCCUPATION"?

Resolution 242 marked the first time that a UN resolution had applied the term "occupation" to the case of Palestine. When Jordan, in 1948, took control of the area now commonly called the West Bank, the term *occupation* was not used. In the past 35 years, a number of UN resolutions have declared Israel to be in belligerent occupation of east Jerusalem, including the Old City, as well as of the territories recovered by Israel in 1967. What is occupation?

Many treatises on the law of war have defined the term "occupied territory." Most of them define "occupation" as an enemy army's presence and control in a particular territory. In recent years, the International Committee of the Red Cross (ICRC) has defined "occupation" as follows: "Under international law, there is occupation when a State exercises non-acquiesced effective control over a territory on which it has no sovereign title." The International Court of Justice (ICJ) has defined another condition that must be present for an occupation to exist. It has determined that "in order for a belligerent occupation to exist the occupying army must actually exercise its authority in the territory, and thereby supplant the authority of the sovereign government of that area."

How applicable are these definitions to Israel—in regards to the West Bank, Gaza, the Sinai, and the Golan Heights? Is it true that Israel has "no sovereign title" to the territories it took control of in 1967? Or does Israel have sovereign title to these territories?

In 1948, Jordan took control of the area now commonly called the West Bank, including East Jerusalem, and held it until 1967.

WHEN JORDAN, IN 1948, TOOK CONTROL OF THE AREA NOW COMMONLY CALLED THE WEST BANK, THE TERM *OCCUPATION* WAS NOT USED.

Golan Heights and Sinai

In regards to the Golan Heights and the Sinai, the conditions of occupation have applied (the Sinai was eventually returned to Egypt) or do apply. The question is whether Israel's occupation of those territories has been legal or illegal. According to international law, a state can legally occupy a territory if it needs to do so in order to maintain the security of its own domain. In other words, it is allowed to continue an occupation if giving up control of the territory in question would present a threat to its own security and peace.

IN REGARDS TO GAZA, ISRAEL GAVE THE TERRITORY TO THE PALESTINIAN PEOPLE IN 2005 IN EXCHANGE FOR A PEACE AGREEMENT. THE GOVERNMENT OF ISRAEL UPROOTED THOUSANDS OF JEWS FROM THEIR HOMES AND FORCED THEM TO MOVE TO ISRAEL IN ORDER TO ADVANCE THE PEACE PROCESS.

This has been the case with the Golan Heights. The Golan Heights is a rocky plateau in the mountains that overlook Syria, Lebanon, and Israel. It is a place from which a hostile army could inflict significant damage on northern Israel. The political circumstances in Syria and Lebanon present threats to Israel's civilian population, and so Israel has maintained control of the Golan Heights for defense and security purposes.

West Bank and Gaza

The case is different with the West Bank and Gaza. Here, the conditions of occupation don't clearly apply. Some international jurists have argued that, since these territories were originally part of the national home prospectively granted to the Jewish people by the Mandate for Palestine, Israel (as the agent of the Jewish people) has the strongest claim of any state to sovereign title over them.

The only other state in history, apart from Israel, that could be considered a sovereign government over the West Bank is Turkey. But Turkey relinquished all claims to sovereignty when its government signed the

The Golan Heights is a strategically important rocky plateau in the mountains that overlook Syria, Lebanon, and Israel.

Treaty of Lausanne on July 24, 1923. Israel, on the other hand, received prospective rights and title to Judea and Samaria (the West Bank) when the League of Nations approved the Mandate for Palestine in July 1922. The Mandate recognized the Jewish people's right to build their national home in Palestine, a territory that included the West Bank. Since 1923, no sovereign government except Israel has had any legal claim to title over the West Bank (which includes all of Jerusalem).

In summary, it is debatable whether Israel's control of the West Bank has constituted an "occupation" under international law. If Israel has sovereign title over the West Bank, then its presence there cannot be classified as an "occupation" in the sense defined by the ICRC.

In regards to Gaza, Israel gave the territory to the Palestinian people in 2005 in exchange for a peace agreement. The government of Israel uprooted thousands of Jews from their homes and forced them to move to Israel in order to advance the peace process. Unfortunately the move was not successful. Since the withdrawal, tens of thousands of rockets have been fired from Gaza at civilian centres in Israel.

Bulldozers and other powerful machinery were used to demolish Jewish settlements in Gaza in 2005 as Israel's unilateral disengagement plan was put into effect and all Israeli citizens were evicted from the area.

THE KHARTOUM CONFERENCE AND THE PLO CHARTER

The Kfar Etzion Kibbutz was built in 1943 on land purchased in the 1930s. It was destroyed, and many of its settlers killed, in the 1948 War. The kibbutz was re-established in 1967.

On June 19, 1967, Israel offered Egypt and Syria the Sinai Peninsula and the Golan Heights, respectively, in exchange for permanent peace treaties. The Arab states rejected the Israeli proposal outright. They did so by way of the Khartoum Resolution. This resolution called for continued belligerency towards Israel. It is famous for containing what became known as the "Three 'No's": "No peace with Israel; no recognition of Israel; no negotiations with it."

Israel responded to the Arab League's Khartoum Resolution with a plan that was named after its author, Yigal Allon, a former general in the IDF. The Allon Plan had two aims: to enable Israel to avoid exercising authority over the Palestinian Arab population in the West Bank; to avoid a return to the insecure pre-1967-war lines. The need to meet these two goals confronted the Israeli government after the Six-Day war and continues to this day.

THE SETTLER MOVEMENT

Included in the Allon Plan was a recommendation that a small number of Jewish settlements be built in sparsely populated areas of the disputed territories, for security purposes. In the decade that followed the 1967 war, some 30 settlements had been established.

The building of Jewish settlements in the disputed territories has been a very contentious issue inside and outside of Israel since its inception. A "settler movement" has pressured successive Israeli governments to remove all restrictions and limitations on settlement building. On the other hand, the Palestinian Authority and the international community, as well as some Israelis, have pressured the Israeli government to stop any settlement building and remove those that have been built, regardless of the security consequences.

By the time of the Khartoum meetings, a number of Palestinian Arab nationalist groups had been established. The most influential of these groups was Harakat al-Tahrir al-Watani al-Filastini (The Palestinian National Liberation Movement), better known by its reverse acronym, Fatah, which means "conquest" in Arabic. In the 1960s, Fatah became—and it remains today—the main Palestinian political party in the West Bank.

Yasser Arafat was one of the founders of Fatah, in 1958, and he led it until his death in 2004. He was an important figure, the face of Palestinian nationalism for half a century. Arafat was born in Cairo, Egypt, in 1929 and studied engineering at an Egyptian university. In Cairo in 1946, he became a volunteer staffer for Haj Amin al Husseini, leader of the Palestine Arabs. (By this point, Husseini had been exiled to Egypt by the British Government for inciting the Arab populations in Palestine to violence and revolt.)

Under Arafat, Fatah would soon become the driving force behind the Palestine Liberation Organization (PLO). The PLO was formed in 1964 at the first Palestine National Council (PNC) meeting, under the instruction and with the approval of the Arab League. The PLO's goal was to mobilize the Palestinian people in opposition to Israel. The Arabs of Palestine, under Arafat's leadership, began to forge a distinct nationalistic identity.

The Palestinian National Covenant, the official Charter of the PLO, was adopted in Cairo in July 1968. This document exhorted its leadership and the Palestinian people to armed struggle and violence against the Jewish state. It advocated liberating Palestine from the state of Israel and establishing Arab hegemony in the entire region—including the area encompass-

---

EXCERPTS FROM THE PALESTINE NATIONAL COVENANT 1968

Article 2: Palestine, with the boundaries it had during the British Mandate, is an indivisible territorial unit. ...

Article 9: Armed struggle is the only way to liberate Palestine. This is the overall strategy, not merely a tactical phase. ...

Article 19: The partition of Palestine in 1947 and the establishment of the state of Israel are entirely illegal, regardless of the passage of time, because they were contrary to the will of the Palestinian people and to their natural right in their homeland, and inconsistent with the principles embodied in the Charter of the United Nations; particularly the right to self-determination. ...

Article 20: The Balfour Declaration, the Mandate for Palestine, and everything that has been based upon them, are deemed null and void. Claims of historical or religious ties of Jews with Palestine are incompatible with the facts of history and the true conception of what constitutes statehood. ...

Article 21: The Arab Palestinian people, expressing themselves by the armed Palestinian revolution, reject all solutions which are substitutes for the total liberation of Palestine. ...

---

ing the State of Israel. Among its basic premises is that Israel has no right to exist. Also noteworthy is the refusal, in Article 20, to acknowledge that Israel has any historical or religious ties to the region.

Hamas, currently the governing Palestinian faction in Gaza, still holds to the provisions of the Covenant and to their premise that all of Palestine, including the territories held by Israel prior to 1967, must be liberated. In other words, Hamas does not acknowledge Israel's right to exist.

THE YOM KIPPUR WAR, THE OIL EMBARGO, AND THEIR EFFECTS

The Yom Kippur War began with a massive and successful Egyptian crossing of the Suez Canal.

On Saturday October 6, 1973, while Israel was engaged in the holy day services of Yom Kippur and the Jewish Sabbath, Egypt and Syria launched a surprise attack on the country's southern front, near the Suez Canal, and on the northern front of the Golan Heights. Many Israeli soldiers on those fronts were not at their usual positions because of the holy day. The first days of the war were dire for the Israelis. By the fifth day, however, Israel had managed to regroup, and the tide turned against the Arab forces. The war ended with a cease-fire on October 24, 1973.

The Arab defeat led to a change in their strategy of aggression toward Israel.

They continued to wage war, but now it was a non-military war. In 1973, members of the Organization of Arab Petroleum Exporting Countries (OAPEC) declared an oil embargo. The "oil weapon" targeted not just the US, but also the industrialized nations of Great Britain, Canada, Japan, and the Netherlands. The Arab states' hope was that the embargo would change these governments' foreign policies towards Israel. The resulting "oil crisis," which started in October 1973, lasted until March 1974.

The strategy was successful. Western Europe and Japan began changing their Middle East policies. For example, Great Britain began refusing to allow the United States to use British bases to airlift supplies to Israel.

The non-military war marked the beginning of a propaganda war on Israel waged by the Arab States.

The first days of the war were dire for the Israelis. By the fifth day, however, Israel had managed to regroup, and the tide turned against the Arab forces.

ENDORSEMENT OF THE PLO

Following the OAPEC oil embargo, there was a crucial meeting of the League of Arab States in Rabat, Morocco, in October 1974. The Rabat Summit brought together the representatives of the PLO and the leaders of 20 Arab states. The Rabat Summit marked the first time that all of the Arab states officially recognized the PLO as the "sole legitimate representative of the 'Palestinian' people." The Arab states also gave official recognition to the PLO's territorial claims to the West Bank.

Following the Rabat Summit, the UN General Assembly took measures that essentially aligned it with the Arab states. First, it made the decision to grant the PLO "Permanent Observer" status. Giving a non-state actor like the PLO such international legitimacy was unprecedented. The UN also established a new permanent committee under the name "Committee on the Exercise of the Inalienable Rights of the Palestinian People." This committee's main task was to make recommendations that would lead to the realization of Palestinian political rights. These rights were now officially recognized by the UN. From this point on, the number of the UN Resolutions targeting Israel increased dramatically, and their tone became more hostile.

UN CONDEMNATION OF ISRAEL

On November 10, 1975, the UN General Assembly adopted Resolution 3379. This resolution declared Zionism to be a form of "racism and racial discrimination." It denounced Israel as the "racist regime in occupied Palestine" whose policies were aimed "at repression of the dignity and integrity of the human being." It associated Israel and Zionism with South African apartheid, colonialism, occupation, and imperialism. This resolution was later revoked by the UN. However, it left a legacy damaging to Israel. For example, there are now annual demonstrations against Israel on university campuses in the US, during what students call "Israel Apartheid Week."

Following the 1973 war and the Arab oil embargo, Israel became the target of more UN sanctions than any other country. Between 1948 and 1982, the UN "condemned," "deplored," or "censured" Israel 38 times. The Arab states were not sanctioned at all. While some approved of this trend, others were troubled by it and saw it as grounds for doubting the UN's neutrality. As one jurist remarked, "Unless one believes that the Israeli–Arab dispute is essentially one between demons and angels, this figure is cause for some concern."

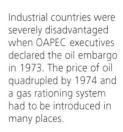

Industrial countries were severely disadvantaged when OAPEC executives declared the oil embargo in 1973. The price of oil quadrupled by 1974 and a gas rationing system had to be introduced in many places.

ACCORD AND DISCORD: 1977–1987

THE CAMP DAVID ACCORDS

Despite continued Arab hostility to Israel, there were steps toward peace. Egyptian President Anwar Sadat's historic and unexpected visit to Jerusalem in 1977 struck a rare positive note in Arab–Israeli relations. Sadat's visit set off widespread protest and demonstrations among other Arab nations and met with strong objections from the PLO.

Despite Arab resistance, Sadat's visit bore fruit. In 1978, meetings took place at Camp David in the United States between Sadat, American President Jimmy Carter, and Israeli Prime Minister Menachem Begin. The agreements concluded at Camp David eventually resulted in the signing of a peace treaty between Israel and Egypt in March 1979, in Washington. In return for the termination of hostilities, Israel agreed to gradually withdraw from the Sinai Peninsula. This set the stage for future land-for-peace strategies by Israel.

The Arab League condemned the Camp David agreements and voted to expel Egypt from the organization. They considered Sadat's actions a betrayal of the joint Israel strategy the Arab states had earlier agreed upon, at Khartoum. In October of 1981, Sadat was assassinated by the Muslim Brotherhood, who publicly opposed Egypt's peace treaty with Israel.

Egyptian President Anwar Sadat (left), American President Jimmy Carter (center) and Israeli Prime Minister Menachem Begin (right) at the Camp David Accords signing ceremony.

UN RESOLUTION 446— ILLEGALITY OF SETTLEMENTS

The late 1970s saw the international community pass further resolutions against Israel. In March 1979—the same month as the Camp David meetings—the UN Security Council adopted Resolution 446. The resolution determined that

> the policy and practices of Israel in establishing settlements in the territories occupied since 1967 have no legal validity and constitute a serious obstruction to achieving a comprehensive, just, and lasting peace in the Middle East.

Although this UN Resolution goes against the legal precedents established by the Mandate for Palestine, it became part of the international community's general attack on Israel's presence in the West Bank (Judea and Samaria) and in Gaza.

ISRAEL'S ANNEXATION OF EAST JERUSALEM AND THE OLD CITY

In July 1980, the Knesset (Israeli Parliament) officially declared its claim to sovereignty over the entire city of Jerusalem, and it annexed the eastern areas, which include the Old City.

Jurists agree that a state cannot unilaterally annex a territory acquired in war and then legitimately claim sovereignty over it. But international law has no provisions which deal with a victor who captures territory to which it previously held prospective title and over which no other sovereign nation had, in the meantime, established a legal claim. In that case, the question concerning annexation is less clear. We need to keep in mind that prospective title to Jerusalem was earlier granted to the Jewish people by the San Remo decisions and by the Mandate for Palestine.

THE PLO IN LEBANON AND JORDAN

While the PLO was gaining political momentum, it was also expanding its paramilitary and terrorist campaign on Israel. In response, with a view to destroying PLO bases, Israel invaded Lebanon in 1982.

The 1982 Lebanon War, though it produced a PLO defeat, had long-term and generally negative consequences for Israel. After the war, the Israeli Defence Force (IDF) maintained a military presence in southern Lebanon. This occupation contributed to the creation of the Iranian-backed Hizballah ("Party of God") party. Israel's hostilities with the PLO in Lebanon ultimately gave way to ongoing conflict with Hizballah fighters in the region.

The PLO defeat in Lebanon led to this organization's adopting a new strategy for Palestinian autonomy in the disputed territories (West Bank and Gaza). The strategy was to piggyback on Jordan's negotiations with Israel. Yasser Arafat and King Hussein of Jordan signed an agreement in February of 1985 pledging a joint Palestinian and Jordanian peace initiative. However, the cooperation between the PLO and Jordan broke down in 1986, and Israel was left without a Jordanian option to solve the Palestinian Arab issue. Israel had hoped that the Palestinians' future could become part of its peace negotiations with the Jordanian state, Jordan being a more stable potential peace partner than the PLO.

In December of 1987, the following year, the situation changed when the Palestinian people themselves initiated an uprising that came to be known as the intifada.

The PLO logo includes a map of Israel with the Palestinian flag above it.

ISRAEL–PALESTINE: 1987 TO THE PRESENT

From 1987 to the present, the socio-political context of Israel-Palestine has featured two closely related dynamics. There have been uprisings, terrorism, and war; and there have been peace proposals.

THE INTIFADA AND ITS AFTERMATH (1987)

On December 9, 1987, a grassroots Palestinian uprising known as the *intifada* (the Arabic term for "shaking off" or "uprising") began in Gaza and spread through the Arab towns and villages of the West Bank (Judea and Samaria). It was intended to pressure Israel and to attract international support for an independent Palestinian state. During the next three years, terrorist attacks killed dozens of Jewish soldiers and civilians. These attacks led, by way of Israeli retaliation, to hundreds of Arab deaths. Injuries on both sides were in the thousands.

A number of factors gave rise to the intifada. One was the perception among Palestinian Arabs, especially the young, that they couldn't count on either the Arab states, Israel, the international community, or their own leadership to resolve their problems.

Yitzhak Rabin, the Israeli minister of defence, tried to crush the rebellion with a harsh iron-fist policy. Israeli forces used rubber bullets and tear gas against demonstrators, imposed curfews, and imprisoned thousands of Palestinian Arabs, including leading activists. These tough measures earned Israel international disapproval as well as domestic stress. By 1987, the world media was portraying Israel as a harsh oppressor, and the Palestinian Arabs as the oppressed.

For the past three decades, the world media has portrayed Israel as a harsh oppressor, and the Palestinian Arabs as the oppressed.

FORMATION OF HAMAS

As the intifada continued, Yasser Arafat's PLO began losing ground in Gaza to a young, fast-growing political faction known as *Hamas* (Arabic for "enthusiasm" or "zeal"). Hamas is an Egyptian-based Muslim Brotherhood movement whose aim is to establish an Islamist Palestinian society. The ideology of Hamas is much more extreme than the secular ideology of Fatah, the dominant faction within the PLO.

PLO ANNOUNCEMENT OF PALESTINIAN STATE (1988)

Conscious of losing support to Hamas among the Palestinian people of Gaza, Arafat announced in 1988 a plan for a two-state solution, with Jerusalem as the Palestinian capital. He included the West Bank and Gaza in his planned Palestinian state. On December 14, he spoke to the UN General Assembly, claiming that the establishment of the State of Palestine is based on the Palestinian Arab people's natural, historic, and legal right to their homeland.

Arafat's contention that the Arabs were entitled to self-determination and sovereignty rights in Palestine according to international law was not—as we have seen—actually in keeping with legal precedent. As previously discussed, the Mandate for Palestine guaranteed the Arab inhabitants of Palestine their civil and religious rights in Palestine, but not political rights of self-determination and sovereignty. Those rights were reserved for the region's prospective Jewish inhabitants.

HAMAS CHARTER

The Hamas Charter includes the following provisions:

Article 11: The Islamic Resistance Movement believes that the land of Palestine is an Islamic Waqf consecrated for future Moslem generations until Judgement Day. It, or any part of it, should not be squandered: it, or any part of it, should not be given up. ...

Article 13: Initiatives, and so-called peaceful solutions and international conferences, are in contradiction to the principles of the Islamic Resistance Movement. ... There is no solution for the Palestinian question except through Jihad [Holy War].

Article 15: It is necessary to instill in the minds of the Moslem generations that the Palestinian problem is a religious problem, and should be dealt with on this basis.

JORDAN'S RESPONSE TO THE INTIFADA

The intifada, as well as having a dismal effect on the economies and daily lives in the disputed territories, intensified the Palestinian refugee problem. It pushed Jordan to sever ties with the Palestinian Arabs.

After the 1948 war, the government of Jordan had extended full Jordanian citizenship to Palestinian Arabs who had taken refuge in Jordan or who had remained in areas of the West Bank controlled by Jordan. (It was the only Arab state to acknowledge the Palestinians in this way.) In the early 1980s, Jordan began to change these citizenship policies. In the intifada's wake, King Hussein of Jordan announced that Jordan was relinquishing its claims to sovereignty over the West Bank and terminating its ties with the Palestinian Arabs living there. Hussein's severing these ties meant revoking their Jordanian citizenship status. Overnight, over 1 million Palestinian Arabs became stateless.

ARAB–ISRAELI NEGOTIATIONS FOR PEACE

THE OSLO ACCORDS (1993)

In September 1993, shortly after Yitzhak Rabin's Labor coalition-led government came to power, secret negotiations began in Oslo, Norway, between Israeli and PLO representatives. The Israelis chose a land-for-peace strategy that had successfully produced the 1982 peace treaty with Egypt. Generally speaking, the plan entailed creating areas of contiguous settlement for Arabs and Jews of the West Bank. This would make security in the territory easier for the Israeli military administration and would create opportunities for Palestinian autonomy.

At the time, almost 90 percent of the West Bank Arab population (1,076,000) lived in or near major Arab cities and towns. The plan proposed that these population centers become Palestinian enclaves. This would allow most Arabs to be released from Israeli control. Following the same principle, 90 percent of the Jews in the West Bank would reside in Jewish enclaves. These Israeli population centers, while located in the West Bank, would become Israeli territory contiguous with the state of Israel. According to the plan, only 10 percent (12,470) of the Jewish population in the West Bank would remain inside Arab enclaves. Jerusalem and the Old City would be under Israeli sovereignty, while Gaza in its entirety would become another Palestinian enclave.

The Israeli Cabinet's approval of this plan was the catalyst for an eight-month period of secret negotiations that resulted in the Oslo Peace Accords. The actual signing of the accords took place at the White

THE OSLO ACCORDS PROVIDED FOR IMMEDIATE PALESTINIAN SELF-RULE IN GAZA AND JERICHO AND AN AGREEMENT ON SELF-GOVERNMENT AFTER THE ELECTION OF A PALESTINIAN COUNCIL.

Oslo is the capital of Norway. The city is also a hub of Norwegian trade, banking, industry and shipping.

House in Washington on September 13, 1993. The signatories were Arafat, Rabin, and Shimon Peres, overseen by U.S. President Bill Clinton.

Four days prior to the signing of the accords, Arafat sent a letter to Rabin stating that the PLO recognized Israel's right to exist in peace and security, committed itself to a peaceful resolution of the conflict, and renounced the use of terrorism and other acts of violence.

In response, Israel agreed to recognize the PLO as the Palestinians' representative in the peace negotiations. The accords provided for immediate Palestinian self-rule in Gaza and Jeri-cho and an agreement on self-government after the election of a Palestinian council.

The accord was essentially an agenda for negotiations, with a five-year plan to transfer authority from Israel to a Palestinian government. During this interim period, further negotiations were to take place that would lead to a "final status" agreement on the remaining issues in the conflict, including the most difficult ones—for example, Jerusalem, refugees, settlements, security arrangements, borders, and relations with other states in the region.

PREAMBLE TO THE OSLO ACCORD'S DECLARATION OF PRINCIPLES

The Government of the State of Israel and the PLO team (in the Jordanian-Palestinian delegation to the Middle East Peace Conference) (the "Palestinian Delegation"), representing the Palestinian people, agree that it is time to put an end to decades of confrontation and conflict, recognize their mutual legitimate and political rights, and strive to live in peaceful coexistence and mutual dignity and security and achieve a just, lasting and comprehensive peace settlement and historic reconciliation through the agreed political process.

The Nobel Peace Prize 1994 was awarded jointly to (left to right) Yasser Arafat, Shimon Peres and Yitzhak Rabin "for their efforts to create peace in the Middle East".

GAZA–JERICHO AGREEMENT (1994)

Following Oslo, Rabin and Arafat met in Cairo. On May 4, 1994, they signed a further agreement, the Gaza–Jericho Agreement, setting the terms of the Israeli forces' withdrawal from Jericho and from parts of the Gaza strip. Under this agreement, the Palestinian Authority (PA) would have legislative, executive, and judicial powers and responsibilities in these regions, including its own armed police force, and it would have control over internal security, education, health, and welfare.

In addition to Israel's withdrawal, the Gaza–Jericho Agreement required commitments from both sides in regards to fostering a relationship of mutual tolerance.

As per the agreement, Israeli troops left Jericho on May 13, and four days later they withdrew from Gaza. Thus the first phase of the agreement had been fulfilled.

For their efforts in support of the Oslo Agreements, the 1994 Nobel Peace Prize was awarded to Rabin, Arafat, and Peres.

ARTICLE 12 OF THE GAZA–JERICHO AGREEMENT: "RELATIONS BETWEEN ISRAEL AND THE PALESTINIAN AUTHORITY"

Israel and the Palestinian Authority shall seek to foster mutual understanding and tolerance and shall accordingly abstain from incitement, including hostile propaganda, against each other and, without derogating from the principle of freedom of expression, shall take legal measures to prevent such incitement by any organizations, groups or individuals within their jurisdiction.

DO ISRAELIS AND PALESTINIANS DESIRE PEACE?

Though the international media has often portrayed Israel as not wanting peace, most Israelis have supported the various efforts to make peace with the Arabs. Some Israelis, however, have doubted whether the Palestinian leadership would ever accept a Jewish state. They have felt that certain approaches to making peace with the Palestinians are naïve and that giving away land to make peace only weakens Israel.

> MOST ISRAELIS HAVE SUPPORTED THE VARIOUS EFFORTS TO MAKE PEACE WITH THE ARABS.

Many Palestinians, too, have responded negatively to the Arab–Israeli agreements. Since the commencement of formal peace talks between the Palestinians and Israel in Oslo in 1993, Hamas has embarked on a campaign of violence and terror.

After the Oslo meetings, Arafat himself, when speaking publicly to Arabs rather than to the Western media, dismissed the peace process as a temporary sacrifice that would ultimately lead to Israel's destruction and to the creation of a Palestinian state in the entire territory. At a South African Mosque in May 1994, he said that the war against Israel would be won not all at once but in phases. One stage would be the acquisition, through "peace" negotiations, of territory from which a military war could then be waged.

ISRAEL–JORDAN PEACE TREATY (1994)

The talks with the PA created momentum for negotiations between Israel and Jordan. These culminated in a peace treaty on October 26, 1994. This treaty, the second between an Arab state and Israel, ended 46 years of hostility between the two nations and has stood to this day.

The treaty provided that Israel and Jordan would recognize and respect each other's sovereignty, territorial integrity, and political independence. It also addressed a host of diverse issues: boundaries, water, police cooperation, the environment, border crossings, refugees, infrastructure, tourism, agriculture, and economic development, among others.

> THE ISRAEL–JORDAN PEACE TREATY ENDED 46 YEARS OF HOSTILITY BETWEEN THE TWO NATIONS AND HAS STOOD TO THIS DAY.

The Oslo II Accord (1995)

Following the initial Oslo agreements, a further agreement—the "Interim Agreement"—was reached on September 28, 1995. Often referred to as the Oslo II Accord, it was to continue the process begun two years earlier with the Oslo Accords and the Gaza–Jericho Agreement. Israel's obligations during this interim period included withdrawing in phases from major Arab areas in the West Bank and the Gaza Strip. To ease the transition of these areas from Israeli to Palestinian administration, the territory was divided up into three areas: Areas "A," "B," and "C."

Area A transferred full civil and security control to the Palestinian Authority (PA). This area includes the Arab cities of Bethlehem, Jenin, Nablus, Qalqilya, Ramallah, Tulkarm, and some 450 villages. In all of these places, Palestinians have self-rule, and there are no Israeli settlements. Entry into this area is strictly forbidden to all Israeli citizens and is currently enforced by Israeli checkpoints and identified by a red sign. The IDF and Israeli police maintain no presence in these areas.

Area B came under Palestinian civil control with joint Israeli–Palestinian security control. It includes Palestinian towns and villages, and areas with no Israeli settlements.

Area C remained under full Israeli security control, but with Palestinians in the area coming under Palestinian civil control and Israelis answering to Israeli civil authority. This area includes all Israeli settlements (cities, towns, and villages), the land in the vicinity of these settlements, and most of the roadways connecting the settlements, as well as strategic areas described as security zones. Jerusalem and the Old City are part of Area C.

The division of the West Bank into Areas A, B, and C was supposed to expire in 1999, at the end of the inter-

Bethlehem is a city located in the central West Bank, about 10 kilometers south of Jerusalem. Since 1995, when Israel ceded it to the PLO, Bethlehem has been governed by the Palestinian Authority.

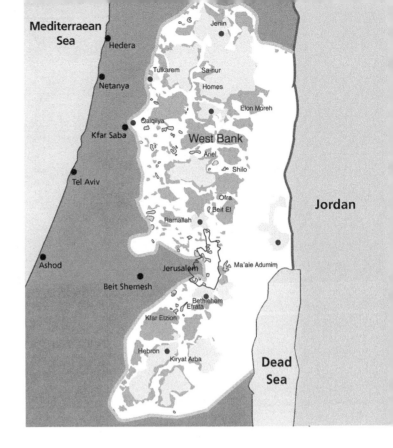

im period. The process did not move forward, however. Israel felt that the Palestinians had not fulfilled their obligations under the Oslo Accord, the following crucial ones in particular: amending the Palestinian National Charter to recognize Israel's right to exist; and promoting peace through changes to the education of their youth, in accordance with Article 12 (quoted on page 90). The Palestinian Authority blamed Israel for the delays, citing its building of settlements in the West Bank as a major obstacle to peace.

The continuing existence of the West Bank's territorial divisions remains a source of contention. Israel still maintains military control of most of the territory and determines unilaterally the particulars of land development within it.

THE CAMP DAVID SUMMIT (2000)

In 2000, Bill Clinton was eager to negotiate a final peace agreement between Israel and the Palestinians before the end of his presidency. He invited Israeli Prime Minister Ehud Barak and PLO Chairman Arafat to Camp David in July of 2000. Meetings in the president's Maryland retreat were held between July 11 and July 24.

During the summit, Clinton presented a proposal to Arafat and his delegation that would have given the Palestinians control of a continuous territory encompassing 91 percent of the West Bank and 100 percent of the Gaza Strip. (The Palestinian

numbers were different; according to their interpretation, the final proposal offered them only 83 percent of the West Bank).

Arafat rejected the offer and submitted no counterproposals. His rejection frustrated many people, including Arabs. Prince Bandar, the Saudi ambassador to the United States, was quoted as saying the following to Arafat: "If we lose this opportunity, it is not going to be a tragedy. This is going to be a crime."

Map of the West Bank Subdivisions.

Area A:
Exclusive Palestinian Control

Area B:
Joint Palestinian Civil/ Israeli Security Control

Area C:
Exclusive Israeli Control

Israeli Settlement

● Palestinian Community

● Israeli Community

▬▬ Pre-1967 Border (The Green Line)

── Jerusalem Municipal Boundaries

Israeli Prime Minister Ehud Barak and Palestinian leader Yasser Arafat shake hands at the White House in Washington during the Camp David Summit. Unfortunately, the summit ended without an agreement.

Police and security personnel inspecting the remains of a burnt-out public transportation bus in Haifa during the intifada. The attacks by militant wings of Fatah and Hamas claimed the lives of 305 men, women, and children, and left hundreds of others maimed or injured.

US President George W. Bush (center), Israeli Prime Minister Ariel Sharon (right) and Palestinian Prime Minister Mahmoud Abbas (left) during the Red Sea Summit in Jordan, in 2003. The purpose of the summit was to boost President Bush's Roadmap for Peace. Despite the pledges of both sides, there was little progress in implementing the Roadmap, as violence continued.

THE AL-AQSA INTIFADA (2000)

Amid the tensions caused by the failed talks at Camp David, Ariel Sharon, then leader of the opposition in Israel, visited the Temple Mount on September 28, 2000. He was accompanied by a small group of Israelis and a large contingent of Israeli police. This visit triggered severe violence and riots throughout the West Bank, the Gaza Strip, and within the Arab communities inside Israel. The Palestinians blamed Sharon's visit for the uprising, which is often referred to as the "Al-Aqsa Intifada." The Israelis, in turn, blamed Arafat, saying that the intifada was planned long before the Temple Mount visit and that it was Arafat's way of deflecting the negative attention he'd received over Camp David.

Despite the escalating violence, peace initiatives continued for the next four years. There were negotiations in January 2001, on the eve of the Israeli elections, in Taba on the Sinai Peninsula. These were followed, in 2002, by another attempt to solve the Israeli–Palestinian conflict—namely, the "Road Map" or Performance-Based Proposal. This came about through the initiatives of the United States, the European Union, Russia, and the UN (collectively referred to as the "Quartet"). This plan involved several phases, and it resembled previous initiatives in the following respects:

- It was based on the principle of land for peace;

- Territorial boundaries would be based on UN resolutions 242 and 338;

- It required of the PA full recognition of Israel;

- It granted Israelis the right to live in peace and security; and

- It required Israel to freeze settlement building in the West Bank.

The peace efforts continued, but so did the violence. The number of suicide bombings in Israel increased from four in 2000 to a peak of 55 in 2002.

THE SECURITY BARRIER (2002)

The attacks by militant wings of Fatah and Hamas claimed the lives of 305 men, women, and children, and left hundreds of others maimed or injured. In 2002, the Israeli government decided to build a security barrier to protect their citizens from the suicide bombings. The barrier became the focus of much negative international attention. Its success in preventing attacks was undeniable, however. As its construction progressed, the number of attacks and casualties dropped by approximately 50 percent each year until, in 2007, there was only one attack.

The security barrier was built by Israel along the 1949 Armistice Line ("Green Line"). The barrier protects civilians from Palestinian terrorism, especially suicide bombing attacks.

HOT TOPIC 2.8
IS THE SECURITY BARRIER JUSTIFIED?

Because the barrier was successful in its practical aims, the majority of Israelis supported its construction. On the other hand, Israeli settlers and Palestinians living on the east side of the barrier were vehemently opposed to it; the barrier interfered with their freedom of movement and their access to services and land.

The UN did not view the barrier as justified and asked the International Court of Justice (ICJ) to rule on its legality. On July 9, 2004, the ICJ issued the following statement: "The Court finds that the construction by Israel of a wall in the Occupied Palestinian Territory and its associated régime are contrary to international law."

The ICJ's opinion stated that the territory upon which the security barrier was built belonged to the Palestinians. International jurist Dr. Jacques Gauthier noted that the ICJ opinion, by failing to consider the earlier legal decisions regarding Pal-

estine (under the Mandate for Palestine, for example) "takes away the rights and entitlements acquired by the Jewish people over the last century."

The ICJ ruling on the security barrier also did not take into consideration Israel's right as a member state of the United Nations to take measures to protect its civilian population, which, in 2002, included not just Jews but over 1 million Arabs.

The graph below shows the effectivness of the barrier in preventing terrorist attacks. As its construction progressed, the number of attacks and casualties dropped by approximately 50 percent each year.

A total of 144 suicide bombing attacks from 2000 to 2007 killed 542 people.

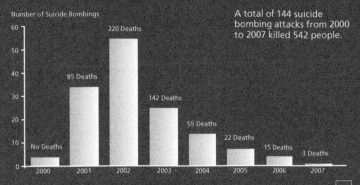

Number of Suicide Bombings

- 2000: No Deaths
- 2001: 85 Deaths
- 2002: 220 Deaths
- 2003: 142 Deaths
- 2004: 55 Deaths
- 2005: 22 Deaths
- 2006: 15 Deaths
- 2007: 3 Deaths

GAZA DISENGAGEMENT 2005

With no end in sight to the problems posed by the Gaza Strip and Hamas, Prime Minister Sharon and Deputy Prime Minister Ehud Ohlmert publicly floated the idea of a withdrawal from Gaza. The plan called for the dismantling of all 21 Jewish settlements in Gaza and the removal of their 8,000-plus settlers, as well as the dismantling of four small settlements in the West Bank. The plan shocked many in Israel and was met with fierce opposition from settlers and from government officials, including some from Sharon's own party. Nonetheless, on February 20, 2005, the Israeli Cabinet voted in favor of it.

At midnight on August 14, Gaza was sealed off, and the settlers who had not already left were given 48 hours to leave voluntarily. There were some minor incidents, but the

The evacuation of the Bedolach settlement was part of the Gaza Disengagement, which took place during the summer of 2005.

withdrawal was carried out peacefully, and the last of the settlements was evacuated on Monday, August 22, 2005.

The majority of Israelis had supported the Gaza withdrawal, hoping that this concession would be a major stepping-stone to both peace and a two-state solution. These hopes have been disappointed. Since 2005, Israeli cities and towns have endured a bombardment of rocket attacks—nearly 12,000 in the past decade—from Hamas and Iranian-backed terrorist groups in Gaza.

THE 2006 LEBANON WAR

While absorbing attacks from Gaza in the west, Israel also had to address hostilities on its northern border. On July 12, 2006, Hizbullah terrorists crossed from Lebanon into Israel and attacked a group of Israeli soldiers patrolling the border, killing eight and kidnapping two others. Israel responded with air strikes aimed at Hizbullah positions inside Lebanon, and Hizbullah unleashed a barrage of Katyusha rockets, targeting civilian population centers in some of Israel's northern cities, including Kiryat Shmona, Haifa, and Safed. They fired more than 100 rockets daily—nearly 4,000 rockets in total—at Israel during this conflict, which lasted close to five weeks.

Israeli and Palestinian officers hold a field situation assessment in preparation for Israel's 2005 Gaza Disengagement.

In retaliation, Israel sought to disable the infrastructure through which Iran and Syria supplied weapons to Hizbullah. For example, Israel bombed Beirut's airport and certain roads and bridges. It also launched a ground offensive aimed at expelling as many Hizbullah terrorists as possible from southern Lebanon.

Hizbullah had occupied southern Lebanon since Israel's withdrawal in 2000 and had attacked Israel more than 20 times with cross-border raids and rockets. They dwelt and held meetings among civilians, and they stored their weapons in civilian houses. They also—in direct violation of international humanitarian law—fired rockets into Israel from civilian neighborhoods.

Faced with these tactics, Israel opted to sacrifice the element of surprise in order to spare innocent lives. In advance of strikes in civilian areas, Israel dropped fliers and sent radio messages warning civilians to leave. Despite these efforts, the strikes against Hizbullah terrorists led to the temporary displacement of 800,000 Lebanese civilians and to the deaths of an es-

timated 1,000 non-Israeli combatants and non-combatants.

The conflict subsided with the adoption of UN Security Council Resolution 1701 on August 11, 2006. It called for a full cessation of the hostilities, for the withdrawal of Israeli forces from Lebanon, and for the "unconditional release of the abducted Israeli soldiers, that have given rise to the current crisis." Hizbullah released the corpses of the two kidnapped soldiers—Ehud Goldwasser and Eldad Regev—to Israel in July 2008, two years after their abduction, as part of a prisoner exchange. Until that time, Hizbullah had refused to provide information about their fate.

Katyusha rocket launched from Lebanon by Hizbullah hits the Bnei-Zion hospital in Haifa, Israel.

Inset: Israel Defense Forces soldiers leaving Lebanon at the end of the war.

IN THE LEBANON WAR ISRAEL OPTED TO SACRIFICE THE ELEMENT OF SURPRISE IN ORDER TO SPARE INNOCENT LIVES.
IN ADVANCE OF STRIKES IN CIVILIAN AREAS, ISRAEL DROPPED FLIERS AND SENT RADIO MESSAGES WARNING CIVILIANS TO LEAVE.

ISRAEL-PALESTINE IN THE NEW MIDDLE EAST

THE GAZA WARS (2009 AND 2014) AND THE FLOTILLA (2010)

Israel has fought two wars in Gaza in the past five years. The first, called Operation Cast Lead, was a three-week armed conflict with Hamas fighters. Israel's intention in entering Gaza was to stop Hamas's rocket fire into Israel and to stop the smuggling of weapons into the Gaza strip. The war began on December 27, 2008 and ended on January 18, 2009 with a ceasefire. Israel and the pro-Palestinian factions, under the scrutiny of the world media and various human rights organizations, accused each other of violating international humanitarian law.

On January 3, 2009, Israel established a naval blockade off the coast of the Gaza Strip as part of its armed conflict with Hamas. In late May 2010, a flotilla of six ships set out from Tur-

Eight Qassam launchers, seven equipped with operating systems and one armed and ready to launch, were uncovered during one of the counter-terrorism operations in northern Gaza. This Qassam rocket attack was intended to target Israel's civilian population.

key for Gaza to protest Israel's naval blockade. The Israeli navy's special forces launched a military operation to enforce the blockade and take control of the ships. The largest ship, the Mavi Marmara, had over 500 passengers on board. Most were unarmed peace activists, but about 40 activists had weapons. The Mavi Marmara was the only ship to ignore radio communications, which forced the IDF to attempt a takeover. During the takeover, IDF soldiers met resistance and were attacked by the armed activists. Some of the armed activists suffered casualties and other passengers were injured. The international media and human rights organizations almost unanimously condemned Israel for its actions in this episode.

The IDF launched the second Gaza war, called Operation Protective Edge, on July 8, 2014. The operation's goals were to restore security to Israeli civilians and to dismantle a sophisticated Hamas tunnel network used to initiate terrorist attacks on Israel. This war came after months of rocket fire from Gaza aimed at some of Israel's most populous cities. Since the beginning of the year, 450 such rockets had been fired. Most were intercepted by Israel's Iron Dome missile defense system. However, their potential for damage was enormous and their hostile intention clear.

Qassam rockets were fired from the Gaza Strip into the Israeli border city of Sderot, which is less than a mile from Gaza. This city has been a continual target of rocket attacks from Gaza since 2001.

HOT TOPIC 2.9
CAN WAR BE JUST?

What is a "just war," and were Israel's operations in Gaza just? Advocates of just-war doctrine hold that war is justifiable under certain conditions but that there are or should be limits on the violence used to fight a war. The doctrine is concerned with two kinds of justice related to war.

The first kind of justice, *jus ad bellum*, involves a set of criteria for determining when it is lawful and moral to enter a war. A just war must

- be a war of last resort, with all other means of resolution explored;

- be authorized by a legitimate authority, either the state or an international organization;

- be waged for a just cause, not from aggression or from a desire for vengeance;

- have a good chance of successfully achieving a desirable outcome (wars fought for good causes that are ultimately hopeless are not justifiable); and

- end in a peace that is preferable to the situation that existed before the outbreak of war.

The second kind of justice involved in just war is called *jus in bello*. It involves a second set of criteria, and they concern the manner in which a war is fought—in other words, how it is conducted. These criteria are as follows:

1. A just war must take into consideration *proportionality*. This means that the positive effects of a military action (of an airstrike, for example) must outweigh its negative consequences (destruction and death). The method and level of violence deployed to fulfill the aims of the mission must pose the lowest possible risk to the civilian population and must take into account the military value of the target.

2. A just war must *discriminate* between combatants and noncombatants; the two must be treated differently. Civilians cannot be the intentional targets of military operations, and civilian casualties, often called collateral damage, must be minimized so far as possible.

The Gaza Wars, like Israel's 2006 conflict in Lebanon, have differed from traditional wars insofar as they have not been between two states. In both cases, Israel has been fighting non-state actors—terrorist organizations such as Hizbullah and Hamas—not bound by the Geneva Conventions concerning the protection of civilians in and around a war zone. Such conflicts are sometimes called asymmetrical wars. The asymmetry of these wars—and the media images of Israel's armed forces in combat with paramilitary fighters dressed as civilians—has brought Israel much condemnation in the international community and media.

A rocket fired from Gaza in June 2014 directly hit a factory in Sderot, setting the building ablaze. The fire led to further explosions inside the factory.

Israel's wars in Gaza have come under considerable scrutiny in the UN and in the international media. After the first Gaza war, the UN produced the Goldstone Report. A scathing document, based on testimony from Palestinians in Gaza, the 500-plus page report accused Israel of intentionally targeting and killing civilians. Its author, Judge Richard Goldstone, charged Israel with numerous human rights abuses, and his conclusions led to allegations of war crimes.

In January 2010, the Israeli government released a response criticizing the Goldstone Report and disputing its findings. The IDF insisted that its armed forces took "extensive measures" to avoid striking noncombatants. These measures included issuing warnings via leaflets, broadcasting warnings in Palestinian media outlets, and placing phone calls to homes in the conflict zone, warning the occupants to leave the area.

The Israeli claims were forcefully supported by Colonel Richard Kemp, a retired British Army officer who commanded forces in Afghanistan and who served with NATO and the United Nations. In October of 2009, Kemp made a presentation to the United Nations Human Rights Council, responding to the Goldstone report. Contesting the report's findings, Kemp maintained that, during its 2008 operation in Gaza,

the Israeli Defence Forces did more to safeguard the rights of

Judge Richard Goldstone led a mission created by the UN Human Rights Council to investigate international human rights and humanitarian law violations related to the Gaza War.

civilians in a combat zone than any other army in the history of warfare. Israel did so while facing an enemy that deliberately positioned its military capability behind the human shield of the civilian population.

Hamas, like Hizbullah, are expert at driving the media agenda. Both will always have people ready to give interviews condemning Israeli forces for war crimes. They are adept at staging and distorting incidents.

During the conflict, the IDF allowed huge amounts of humanitarian aid into Gaza. To deliver aid virtually into your enemy's hands is, to the military tactician, normally quite unthinkable. But the IDF took on those risks.

In 2011, Judge Goldstone recanted his earlier judgment. He wrote that he no longer believed that Israel intentionally targeted civilians in Gaza.

Israel's wars with Hamas in Gaza and Hizbullah in Lebanon are the latest in what is now nearly a century of struggle between Arabs and Jews in Israel-Palestine. What are the main challenges and opportunities currently facing these peoples? Where do they go from here?

In October 2009, Colonel Richard Kemp made a presentation to the United Nations Human Rights Council in response to the Goldstone report. He said that "during Operation Cast Lead, the Israeli Defense Forces did more to safeguard the rights of civilians in the combat zones than any other army in the history of warfare."

PART THREE

ISRAEL-PALESTINE TODAY: CHALLENGES AND OPPORTUNITIES

WHERE DOES ISRAEL-PALESTINE GO FROM HERE? WHAT CHALLENGES AND OPPORTUNITIES FACE THIS REGION'S PEOPLES NOW AND IN THE YEARS AHEAD? FOR THE FORESEE-ABLE FUTURE, ISRAELIS AND ARABS MUST CLOSELY COEXIST. AS WE PONDER THIS INEVITABILITY, WHAT FACTORS MUST BE CONSIDERED? WHAT OPTIONS ARE AVAILABLE?

ISRAEL-PALESTINE: CHALLENGES

Members of the international community continue to demand that Israel resolve the Israeli–Palestinian impasse. Most favour one solution in particular, the two-state solution. Among the challenges now facing Israel is to determine whether this solution is consistent with national security, in a region where sharp ideological divisions exist among peoples and states. Israel-Palestine faces other challenges, too. It must address the question whether the Arab refugees from the 1948 and 1967 wars should be granted a right of return, and the question whether Jerusalem should be a shared capital.

SECURITY AND THE TWO-STATE SOLUTION

Most members of the international community believe that negotiations between Israel and the Palestinians should result in two states. And they believe that the borders of Israel and Palestine should be based on the pre-1967 lines, but with mutually agreed swaps, so that secure and recognized borders are established for both states.

Prior to 1967, the eastern boundary of Israel was the 1949 Armistice Line—the Green Line. Under the Armistice Agreement, the Green Line was never supposed to be the basis for borders. However, it has become the line by which the international community demarcates Israel's future borders according to the two-state solution. With these borders, Israel would be 9 miles wide at its narrowest point. The combined width of Israel and the West Bank, from the Mediterranean to the Jordan River, averages about 40 miles.

Israel's security concern about the two-state solution is that the territorial concessions involved would weaken the country's defence systems. For example, Israel would lose the early-warning stations that alert the country in the event of attacks from the east.

Arab States

Proposed Palestinian Arab State

Haifa

Mediterraean Sea

Narrowest point
15Km 9.3 mile

Tel Aviv

Jerusalem

Beersheba

Mediterraean Sea

Adjacent Coastal Plain
70% of Israel's Population
80% of Industrial Capacity

Ramat David Airbase
17 Km
10.5 Mile

Jenin

14 Km
8.7 Mile

Netanya   Tulkarem

0.7 Km
0.4 Mile

Kfar Saba   Qalqiliya

20 Km
Sde Dov Airport   12.4 Mile
Tel Aviv

Ben-Gurion
Intl. Airport   Rantis

900 m
3,000 ft
Above Sea Level

9.5 Km
5.9 Mile

Ashod

Tel Nof Airbase

Ashkelon   Jerusalem

0.4 Km
0.25 Mile

Hazor Airbase   Betlehem

Gaza Strip

17 Km
10.5 Mile

Beer Shiva   20 Km
12.4 Mile

Nevatim Airbase

The two-state solution presents serious security challenges for Israel and its citizens—Arab and Jewish citizens both. It would leave the country vulnerable to today's advanced weaponry. Israel is a small state surrounded by countries historically hostile to it. Certain of the neighboring territories are home to terrorist organizations that are sponsored by Iran and Qatar and committed to Israel's destruction.

What happens if the territory proposed for a Palestinian state—namely, Judea and Samaria (the West Bank)—should fall under the control of radical factions, as has happened in Gaza? The Jordan Rift Valley on Israel's eastern frontier, which lies within the eastern portion of the West Bank, is strategically vital because it includes what is now Israel's border with Jordan. That border, if surrendered to Palestinian control, could become, with respect to national security, equivalent to the border between Gaza and Egypt.

When Israel withdrew from Gaza in 2005, a terrorist infiltration of the region ensued, along with the influx of hundreds of tons of ammunition and weaponry (rockets and mortars). These rockets and mortars were subsequently launched at Israeli civilians. Israel's withdrawal from the Jordan Valley

would expose the country to the same threats it now faces from Gaza. But there would be an added threat because of the mountain ridge in Judea and Samaria.

Forces hostile to Israel could use the mountain ridges in Judea and Samaria (the West Bank) as rocket-launching stations.

WITH THE TWO-STATE SOLUTION BORDERS, ISRAEL WOULD BE 9 MILES WIDE AT ITS NARROWEST POINT. THE TWO-STATE SOLUTION PRESENTS SERIOUS SECURITY CHALLENGES FOR ISRAEL AND ITS ARAB AND JEWISH CITIZENS.

If Judea and Samaria (the West Bank) were to become a Palestinian state, much of the mountain ridge would be under Palestinian control. This mountain ridge—the spine of which runs north–south and parallel to Israel's coast for 70 kilometers—rises up to 3,000 feet and overlooks Israel's major coastal cities. These cities contain more than 70 percent of Israel's population, 80 percent of its industry, and all of its airports and seaports. All of this would come under the threat of rocket attacks.

From the mountain ridge, a hostile force deploying advanced weaponry could hit virtually any point in Israel. Most of the country's population and infrastructure would be in easy range of rockets, as would the Trans-Israel Highway, Israel's National Water Carrier, the Hadera power plant, and Israel's military bases. Ben-Gurion Airport—Israel's only international airport—would be especially vulnerable, in range of even primitive rockets or shoulder-launched anti-aircraft missiles. All planes taking off and landing would be under constant threat. In short, it would be impossible to defend the State of Israel.

The two-state solution poses a significant challenge for Israel. How is the country to meet its security needs while making room on its doorstep for another state, in all likelihood a hostile one? How can defensible borders be established in the narrow strip of land between the Jordan River and the Mediterranean?

Topographical map of Israel showing the varying elevations of the country's landmass.

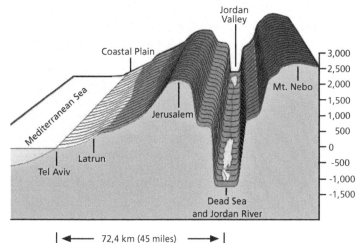

A view of Tel Aviv from the West Bank. From the mountain ridge, a hostile force could hit virtually any point in Israel. Ben-Gurion Airport (inset)—Israel's only international airport—would be in range of even primitive rockets or shoulder-launched anti-aircraft missiles.

THE RIGHT OF RETURN FOR ARAB REFUGEES

Another challenge for Israel-Palestine is the Palestinian Authority's claim that Arab refugees from the 1948 and 1967 wars have a right to return to Israel. Today, millions of Arabs are living in refugee camps in the Middle East. The majority of them are descendants of Arabs who fled their homes in Palestine during the 1948 war. Though most of them were not born in Israel, they identify themselves as Palestinian and claim a right to return to Israel and to be compensated by Israel for the losses suffered 65 years ago.

The refugees have long been encouraged in this claim by the Arab governments hosting them. With the exception of Jordan, these governments have refused to absorb or naturalize their stateless Arab brothers. As a result, many in the camps live in dreadful conditions, disadvantaged and marginalized by the established Arab citizenry.

The original basis for the Arab claim of a "right to return" is Resolution 194, passed by the UN on 11 December 1948. A year later, the United Nations established the United Nations Relief and Aid Works Agency for Palestine Refugees in the Near East (UNRWA).

Arab refugees leaving Israel-Palestine in 1948. Israel has offered to pay compensation to the actual refugees from 1948 so that they can settle either in the Arab states where they currently reside or in the West Bank and Gaza.

ISRAEL-PALESTINE TODAY: CHALLENGES AND OPPORTUNITIES

Bird's-eye view of the Za'atri camp for Syrian refugees, run by the UNHCR. This UN agency's aim is to make refugee status a temporary condition, with a refugee population naturalized over time by a new host country.

UNRWA is a UN agency separate from the United Nations High Commissioner for Refugees (UNHCR), also known as the UN Refugee Agency. The latter agency deals with all other refugees, such as (in the contemporary context) the Christians, Yazidis, and other minorities fleeing IS (Islamic State).

The UNHCR oversees the resettlement of refugees in new lands, enabling them to make new lives for themselves. This UN agency's aim is to make refugee status a temporary condition, with a refugee population naturalized over time by a new host country. Under the UNHCR model refugee status does not get passed on to subsequent generations. The refugee population does not swell by the year. Had the UNHCR been in charge of the Arab refugees and their resettlement, there would be virtually no Palestinian refugees today. Like almost all other refugees of the past 100 years, they would have been successfully resettled and absorbed over time into other populations.

UNRWA's definition of a refugee and its approach to the problems of a refugee population differ remarkably from those of the UNHCR. According to the UNRWA, anyone who lived in Israel-Palestine from 1946 to 1948 qualifies as a refugee. If he is male, his descendants also qualify as refugees no matter where they are born. UNRWA's unswerving aim is to return the refugees to Israel rather than to resettle them in a new host country. Under the UNRWA definition

UNHCR headquarters are located in Geneva, Switzerland.

Granting these Arab refugees a right of return would pose an obvious challenge for Israel. If the UNRWA definition of *refugee* is accepted, Israel would be required to absorb as many as 7 million people, a number almost equal to Israel's current population. This challenge would be insurmountable.

For this reason, Israel has rejected the Palestinian Authority's claim of a right to return. Instead, it has offered to pay compensation to the *actual* refugees from 1948 (not to their descendants, born in other countries) so that they can settle or re-settle either in the Arab states where they currently reside or in the West Bank or in Gaza.

and policy, the number of Arab refugees has grown from an estimated 750,000 in 1948 to 7 million today. This population continues to grow every year and will continue to grow in perpetuity.

The UNRWA receives billions of dollars annually for the Palestinian refugees, mostly from Europe and the United States. Much of this benefits the Palestinian Authority and Hamas. UNRWA employs about 30,000 people, many of whom are also on the Palestinian Authority and Hamas payroll. UNRWA facilities, such as schools, have been used for many years as warehouses for rockets. UNRWA hospitals double as command centres for terrorist attacks.

Many in Israel hold that the Arabs themselves, not just Israel, must assume some responsibility for the refugees created by the 1948 war. This war was initiated by the Arab states, after all (see "The 1948 War and It's Legacies," in Part II), and the Arabs were not the only refugees created by it. Approximately 800,000 Jews were expelled, without compensation, from Arab countries where they had been living for centuries and in some cases millennia. The vast majority of those Jewish refugees were absorbed by Israel decades ago.

Jewish Immigrants from Iraq leaving the Lod Airport (presently the Ben-Gurion Airport) in 1951. Approximately 800,000 Jews were expelled from Arab countries where they had been living for centuries. The vast majority of those Jewish refugees were absorbed by Israel decades ago.

Beitar Illit is an Israeli settlement in the Judaean Mountains of the West Bank.

JEWISH SETTLEMENTS

One of the most challenging issues facing Israel-Palestine concerns the Jewish settlements in Judea and Samaria (the West Bank).

After the 1967 War, Israel began to build Jewish settlements in Judea and Samaria. It did so for various reasons, including security (see page 80). By 1977, about 30 Jewish settlements had been established. By the late 1980s, this number had increased significantly.

The UN has passed a number of resolutions condemning the settlements. In 1979, it characterized them as illegal under international law (see page 85). In 2004, The International Court of Justice (ICJ) expressed the view that Israeli settlements in Judea and Samaria (West Bank) were a violation of the Fourth Geneva Convention. Article 49 of the Convention, adopted after WWII, says that an occupying power is prohibited from deporting or transferring parts of its own population into a territory that it occupies. Israel does not consider the Convention applicable to Judea and Samaria, or to any part of Jerusalem. They argue that the concept of occupation does not apply to these areas (see pages 77-79) and that the Geneva Convention properly refers to forced transfers, such as the transfers imposed by the Nazis in WWII Europe, not the voluntary decisions made by Israeli citizens to live in Judea and Samaria.

The international community and the ICJ continue to view Jewish settlements as a violation of the Fourth Geneva Convention and as a major roadblock to peace. The Boycott, Divest and Sanction (BDS) movement holds that settlements are among the main reasons for its anti-Israel policies.

Today, there are some 121 settlements, with about 187,000 Israelis living in the West Bank (among about 1.5 million Arabs), 20,000 in the Golan Heights, and over 200,000 in areas of Jerusalem beyond the 1967 borders (Green Line). The vast majority of Israelis who live beyond the 1967 lines reside in neighborhoods and suburbs of Jerusalem and Greater Tel Aviv. These areas are densely populated but geographically quite small. Israel has taken the position that any realistic peace agreement must allow these large Jewish population centres (settlements), as well as other places of strategic and national importance, to be incorporated into the final borders of Israel.

Although Israel has never agreed that the Fourth Geneva Convention applies to the West Bank, the Israeli government promised, in its 1993 Oslo Agreement with the PLO, to prohibit the creation of new settlements and to halt the expansion of existing ones until peace negotiations with the Palestinian Authority were completed. However, since 1993, the PA has continued to reject peace proposals presented by Israel and the international community, and has violated its commitments under the Olso Accords. The PA policy of rejection is consistent with nearly fifty years of Arab leaders' refusing to accept any two-state proposal presented to them.

Israel, for its part, has continued to build settlements. The Israeli claim is that the Arab leaders themselves, by refusing peace and by making demands that Israel cannot reasonably meet, are ensuring the continued existence and growth of the settlements.

The PA is demanding that, under any peace agreement, all settlements must be dismantled and all Jews expelled from the West Bank. These demands have received widespread support not only from the international community but from many Israelis.

The government of Israel's response is that, with these demands, the PA is intentionally thwarting the peace process: the PA knows very well that Israel cannot dismantle the larger settlements, such as the Maale Adumim and Betar Ilit. These are home to tens of thousands of people. Israel's current position is that any future peace agreement must reflect the dramatic demographic changes that have occurred since 1967 and must address Israel's security needs. They will not return to the indefensible pre-1967 lines.

Most of the international community questions the Israeli stance, and supports the PA demands for a Palestinian state on land that was originally allocated for the Jewish national home. It also accepts the PA's terms—Jews now settled in Judea and Samaria must be expelled from the prospective Palestinian state and stripped of their rights. In other words, the rights that Israel now grants to its 1.5 million Arab citizens will not be granted to any Jew living in the new Palestinian state.

Ma'ale Adumim is an Israeli settlement in the West Bank. It is located seven kilometers from Jerusalem. More than 40,000 residents live in Ma'ale Adumim, which acquired the status of a city in 1991.

DIVIDING JERUSALEM

Millions of people travel to and around Jerusalem every year, including tourists, Israeli Arabs, and Jews. Although many Arabs who live in the eastern neighborhoods of the city use the modern Light Rail rapid transit line get to their jobs, other Palestinian Arabs have rejected it to protest Israel's presence in the eastern areas of Jerusalem, which they consider the future capital for their Palestinian state.

The Palestinian Authority has demanded that, under any agreement it makes with Israel, Jerusalem must become a shared capital—the capital of the new Palestinian state as well as Israel's capital. In all of its 3000-plus-year history, the city has never been divided in this way except during the 19 years of Jordanian occupation after the 1948 War. Dividing the city according the PA's plan, with east Jerusalem for the Arabs and west Jerusalem for the Jews, would constitute a major challenge for Israel-Palestine.

The demographic basis for such a division is questionable. Prior to 1967, not many Arabs lived in eastern Jerusalem. It was only after the Six Day War, when Israel captured the city from the Jordanians, that hundreds of thousands of Arabs moved there and built thousands of homes. Why did they move there? Most likely they were drawn—like the Arabs who,

at the beginning of the 20th century, poured into Israel-Palestine from all over the Middle East—by the promise of a higher standard of living.

Today, 270,000 Arabs and well over 200,000 Jews live in the mosaic of neighborhoods called East Jerusalem. Jewish and Arab neighborhoods overlap and their urban infrastructures, built by Israel, are fused. They share water systems, sewage pipelines, electricity networks, and vital arteries of transportation. It is doubtful whether dividing Jerusalem is technically feasible.

The Arab and Jewish residents of East Jerusalem share not only an urban infrastructure but also medical and welfare facilities, academic institutions, shopping centers, and recreation sites. Many of the Arabs living there work in Israel and would prefer to remain under Israel's governance rather than come under the PA's. When Israel began to construct the security fence in 2000, some 70,000 Arab residents left their homes in the West Bank to ensure they would remain under Israeli rule.

A divided Jerusalem would present other challenges, too, including a substantial security risk. East Jerusalem could become what Gaza has become since the Israeli withdrawal in 2005—a staging ground for attacks on Israel and a magnet for regional terrorist groups such as Hamas and Hizbullah. The local topography makes this possibility especially disconcerting for residents and tourists.

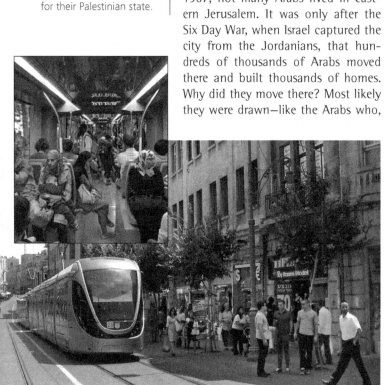

Jerusalem is surrounded by hills that overlook the city's major access routes and the Old City's most important Jewish and Christian holy sites. In 1967, the Jordanian Army exploited the terrain around Jerusalem to launch some 9,000 artillery shells into the city's Jewish neighborhoods. Today, the hills around Jerusalem are home to Arab towns and villages. The Arab village of Beit Iksa, for example, is only a few hundred yards from the main Jerusalem–Tel Aviv highway. This is the main transportation artery connecting Israel's two largest cities.

With a divided Jerusalem, everybody in west Jerusalem, resident or tourist, would be under threat. During 2000 and 2001, before the security fence was completed, there were hundreds of gunfire and mortar attacks on the Gilo neighborhood in southern Jerusalem. These attacks came from Beit Jalla, an Arab town 1,000 feet away. In a divided Jerusalem, Jewish neighborhoods that are only metres away from Arab neighborhoods in eastern Jerusalem would be at risk.

Apart from its physical dangers, a divided Jerusalem would compromise the freedom of worship in the city for Christians as well as Jews. Citizens of Jerusalem and the city's many visitors now move freely through the entire city. Whether this could continue in a divided Jerusalem is doubtful. Recent history argues otherwise. Between 1948 and 1967, when east Jerusalem was under Jordanian Arab rule, there was no such freedom of movement.

Holy sites that have come under PA control since the Oslo Accords have become dangerous for Jews and Christians to visit. The only time in history that all residents of Israel—Christians, Muslims, and Jews—have enjoyed freedom of religion in Jerusalem has been under Israeli sovereignty. Such freedom, like other freedoms, tends to be quite restricted under Arab governments in the Middle East. These governments, both state and non-state (for example, the PA and Hamas), have ideological world views that are very different from Israel's.

A divided Jerusalem would present other challenges, too, including a substantial security risk. Jerusalem is surrounded by hills that overlook the city's major access routes. In 1967, the Jordanian Army exploited the terrain around Jerusalem to launch some 9,000 artillery shells into the city's Jewish neighborhoods.

Freedom House is an NGO that measures freedom in the world in terms of two broad categories: political rights and civil liberties. Freedom House considers Israel's Arab and Jewish citizens to be the only free people in the Middle East and North Africa.

Map of Freedom 2014

■ Free Countries

□ Partly Free Countries

■ Not Free Countries

IDEOLOGY

The State of Israel is a Western-style democracy trying to survive in a region dominated by anti-democratic ideology. This creates tensions above and beyond those arising from the territorial issues between Israel, the PA, and the Arab governments in the region. The international community usually downplays these ideological factors and their role in the current struggles. And yet, arguably, the greatest challenge facing Israel today is how to reconcile its own liberal democratic ideology with the ideologies—anti-democratic and, in some instances, oppressively theocratic—that underpin the Arab societies in the region.

THE GREATEST CHALLENGE FACING ISRAEL TODAY IS HOW TO RECONCILE ITS OWN LIBERAL DEMOCRATIC IDEOLOGY WITH THE ANTI-DEMOCRATIC IDEOLOGIES THAT UNDERPIN THE ARAB SOCIETIES IN THE REGION.

ISRAELI DEMOCRACY IN AN ANTI-DEMOCRATIC MIDDLE EAST

What do we mean by the phrase "liberal democratic society"?

In a Western liberal democracy, citizens are considered to be relatively equal in value, and they expect to have a say in how they are governed. The rule of law prevails in these societies, and their courts are free from government interference. There is also a separation of church and state; religion and the law are separate systems. Perhaps the most crucial feature of a liberal democracy is that its citizens enjoy certain rights, freedoms, and protections, which are usually enshrined in a constitution. These rights and freedoms typically include the right to life, security, privacy, equal treatment, and the right to a fair trial. Liberal democracies are pluralistic and tolerant; their citizens enjoy a free press and free speech, freedom of assembly and petition, and freedom of religion. These are the main features of Western liberal democratic ideology. And they are features of Israel today.

These values are alien to most regimes in today's Middle East. They are alien to the regimes in Iran and in the neighboring Arab states, as well as to the PA in the West Bank and to Hamas in Gaza. These governments are composed of either dictators, wealthy oligarchies, military dictatorships, monarchies, or theocracies. While the levels of authoritarianism and Islamism vary from state to state in the Middle East, the regimes have one thing in common: they exert far more control over their citizens' private lives than the governments in liberal democracies do. People living under the more extreme Islamist regimes—Hamas, IS (Islamic State), and the Iranian Supreme Council, for example—are required to abide by whatever version of strict Islamic law that the governing regime subscribes to. They enjoy few of the rights and freedoms extended to the citizens of Europe, North America, and Israel.

A question facing Israel-Palestine, and potentially one of its major challenges, is the question facing the entire Middle East. It is the question whether the various neighbouring state and non-state actors can accept and eventually embrace a tolerant and pluralistic world view. If they can do this, the prospects for peace within Israel-Palestine and in the region may be realised. To do so, however, these actors will need to do more than just relinquish their authoritarian political principles; they will need to address their fundamental ideologies, in which authoriarian, racist, and anti-Semitic elements, entrenched for centuries, continue to subsist.

Maajid Nawaz, in his autobiography *Radical*, explains how Islamism differs from Islam.

ISLAM AND ISLAMISM

Maajid Nawaz was once a senior member of the Islamist organization *Hizb al-Tahrir* (HT). He left the organization and started a movement to counter Islamist extremism among Muslim youth. In place of this extremism, or Islamism, Nawaz promotes liberal democracy, human rights, and pluralism. His organization, *Khudi*, helps young Muslims break away from the Islamist ideologies that he believes have hijacked their religion and are crippling their societies and progress.

In his autobiography *Radical* (2013), Nawaz explains how *Islamism* differs from *Islam*. The latter, as Nawaz explains, is a religion practiced by over 1.5 billion people around the world. Like most religions, Islam has different sects, ranging from the secular to the devout. Islamism, on the other hand, is primarily an authoritarian political ideology, not a religion. Islamist ideology seeks to impose *shar'ia* (Islamic law) on a society. The religious framework of Islamism is incidental to its political bases. As Nawaz explains, Islamism isn't a religious movement with political consequences; it's a political movement with religious consequences.

As a political project, Nawaz says Islamism was inspired by European fascism, with which it shares many features, including totalitarianism and racism. The militant strand of Islamism, *Jihadism*, fuses Islamism with a literalist religious approach. This fusion is the basis of groups such as al-Qaeda and the Islamic State (IS).

ISRAEL-PALESTINE: FUTURE OPPORTUNITIES

ISRAELIS

The peoples of Israel-Palestine face daunting challenges, but their future is rich in possibility, too. In its six decades of existence, despite war, terrorism, and international disfavour, Israel has grown from a fledgling state with minimal resources, financially overwhelmed, to the 19th ranked country in the world on the UN's Human Development Index (2013). It is now a world leader in water technologies, biomedical technologies, and hi-tech. Products developed by Israeli companies are solving some of the most important issues facing the planet today. The country has the third largest group of corporations represented on the NASDAQ stock exchange in New York, with only the United States and China ranking higher. Israel's free trade agreements with the European Union, the United States, Turkey, Canada, Jordan, and Egypt have made it an important global trading partner. Recent discoveries of large natural gas reserves off its coast could soon make Israel a leading energy exporter in the region. Even its tourist industry is thriving, with over 3.5 million visitors in 2013.

ARABS

Many people, when they look at Israel's success, see it as having come at Arab expense. But the over 1 million Arabs who are citizens of Israel have shared in the country's prosperity. There is no sector of Israeli public life—business, government, law, sport, education, and the military—that Arabs do not participate in. Many Arab-Israelis voluntarily serve in the Israel Defense Forces, some as officers.

For the Arabs in Israel-Palestine who are living under the PA, the future holds opportunity, too, though its form is unclear. In the past, these territories experienced a sustained period of growth and opportunity. The people have known a better life than they know now.

IBM building in Petah Tikva, Israel. The country has a high concentration of high-tech industries located mostly in the coastal plain area. The area is called the Silicon Wadi after the Silicon Valley in California, USA. Silicon Wadi is considered second in importance only to its Californian counterpart

116

For the Arabs in Israel-Palestine who are living under the PA, the future holds opportunity, too, though its form is unclear. Some 70,000 Arab residents left their homes in the West Bank to ensure they would remain under Israeli rule.

In the years immediately following the 1967 war, when Israel recovered the West Bank from Jordan, the Israelis encouraged and financed economic development in the region. By the end of 1970, Arab unemployment in the West Bank had dropped from 12 percent to 3 percent. By 1972, 600,000 Arabs from the West Bank found their daily employment in Israel, and 44,000 Arabs who had fled from the West Bank in 1967 had returned.

From 1969 to 1979, the economy of the West Bank and Gaza grew at a rate of 30 percent a year. It was the fourth-fastest growing economy in the world. Close to 2,000 industrial plants, employing almost half of the region's workforce, were established in the territories during this time. The territories stopped depending on foreign aid, and business activity and standards of living increased dramatically. The population in the West Bank and Gaza grew from roughly 1 million to almost 3 million, and some 261 new towns arose. Facilities for higher education kept step with the economy. In 1967, there were no universities in the West Bank and Gaza, but by the early 1990s, there were seven.

Things began to go wrong in the territories after Yasser Arafat returned from his exile in Tunisia, in 1994. Arafat shifted the Palestinian economy from a growth dynamic, driven by entrepreneurs, to a model whereby foreign aid was delivered to the PLO. The economy clearly suffered from these policies.

According to the World Bank, the economy of the West Bank shrank by some 40 percent in the first five years of the new century. By 2004, the economy in Gaza was much worse off than that of the West Bank. This decline occurred despite a massive influx of foreign aid—to the tune of billions of dollars annually—to the PA.

The future could hold promise for the Arabs of Israel-Palestine. But much will depend on the direction their leadership takes.

THE FUTURE COULD HOLD PROMISE FOR
THE ARABS OF ISRAEL-PALESTINE.
BUT MUCH WILL DEPEND ON THE DIRECTION
THEIR LEADERSHIP TAKES.

CONCLUSION

The land of Israel-Palestine has figured large in human consciousness since the beginning of civilized life on earth. To the great empires of the ancient past—Egypt, Assyria, and Babylon—it was a place of strategic importance, a juncture for trade and a springboard for imperial conquest and control. In time it became the cherished homeland, divinely promised and in time possessed, of the Israelites. Their story, told in the Bible and essential to three of the world's great religions, has shaped the spiritual course of the world. The jewel of this land is Jerusalem, site of the Temple Mount, of the Church of the Holy Sepulchre, and of the Dome of the Rock. In European maps of five hundred years ago, Jerusalem was shown as the hub of the world.

All the maps have been redrawn since then. Old empires have vanished, new ones rising in their stead. And yet Israel-Palestine, that narrow strip of land, still lays an insistent claim to the world's regard. It remains central, sacred to half the peoples of the world, still the subject of strong territorial passions. It is contested no less fiercely today than it was in past millennia, by Israelites and Philistines, by Babylonians and Persians, by Islamic caliphates and European crusaders. Now as then, its affairs and its destiny preoccupy us.

The Jewish people who now possess the land have an ancient claim to it. Their modern title to Israel-Palestine, though challenged and deplored in some quarters, is rooted in history and justified by international law. However, from the moment it was ceded to them, the Israelis have had to defend this right of ownership continually, by argument and by military force. Their struggle is ongoing. The main opponent is another ancient Semitic people, the Arabs, who have a long history in the region and a determined wish to make the land their own.

The Arab states, having started the wars that displaced the Palestinian Arabs from their homes in 1948, have kept them in camps for over 60 years, refusing them citizenship in their own lands. Many in the international community view the Palestinian Arabs with sympathy, and some sympathy is justified. Neither their leaders nor their Arab brothers have served this people well. On this point, many in the international community and the media are silent. They support the Arab regimes, blaming Israel alone for the region's problems and for the

Jerusalem's hills and valleys have been central to the 4,000 year old story that continues to this day.

Palestinian Arabs' plight. The facts of history do not corroborate this blame.

History tells us that, a century ago, the entire Middle East was Ottoman territory. The Allied Powers, having seized this territory from the defeated Turks at the end of World War I, bestowed most of it on the Arabs. This gave them statehood in virtually all of the Middle East. What they weren't given was Israel, the small portion of land the Allied Powers set aside as a prospective state for the Jewish people. The Arabs accepted those of the Allied Powers' decisions that were to their benefit, but refused any benefit to Israel. Their refusal, in the form of violent opposition, continues to this day.

As a result, Israel-Palestine faces major challenges today. The international community regards the two-state solution, with borders based on the 1949 Armistice Line and Jerusalem divided, as the only way of ending the Arab–Israeli impasse. This solution poses an enormous security risk for Israel. The international pressure to accept it is among Israel's contemporary challenges, as is the pressure to absorb millions of potentially hostile Arab refugees, descendants of those dislodged from Israel-Palestine by the 1948 war. Another challenge facing Israel today stems from its being the only democratic state in a region increasingly overrun by authoritarian, anti-democratic ideologies.

The discourse surrounding the modern State of Israel is too often shaped by partisan passions and by facile, simplified perspectives. A person who wishes to avoid these traps must carefully sift the grounds, historical, religious, and legal, of the Arab and the Israeli claims to the land. Critical thinking is crucial, and so is knowledge. A clear-eyed consideration of its long and intricate history, from ancient roots to the present day, is the key to grasping the challenges that confront Israel-Palestine. And it is the key to appraising the possible solutions.

CRITICAL THINKING IS CRUCIAL, AND SO IS KNOWLEDGE. A CLEAR-EYED CONSIDERATION OF ISRAEL-PALESTINE'S LONG AND INTRICATE HISTORY IS THE KEY TO GRASPING THE CHALLENGES THAT CONFRONT THIS REGION.

ISRAEL-PALESTINE TODAY: CHALLENGES AND OPPORTUNITIES

REFERENCES

PART 1

Page 7:   [El Amarna Letters] H.H. Ben Sasson, ed., *A History of the Jewish People*, (Cambridge: Harvard University Press, 1976), 9.

Page 9:   [quotation re protohistory] H.H. Ben Sasson, ed., *A History of the Jewish People*, (Cambridge: Harvard University Press, 1976), 28.

Page 10–11: [Egyptian decline] H.H. Ben Sasson, ed., *A History of the Jewish People*, (Cambridge: Harvard University Press, 1976), 23.

Page 26:   Arabs move West to flee Mamelukes] Caroline Glick, *The Israeli Solution* (New York: Crown Forum, 2014), 190.

Page 34:   [quotation from Herbert Samuel's 1925 report] Martin Gilbert, *The Routledge Atlas of the Arab Israeli Conflict*, 9th ed. (London: Routledge, 2008), 12.

Page 35:   [quotation from Golda Meir] Golda Meir, *My Life* (New York: Dell, 1975), 79.

PART 2

Page 46:   [excerpt from the McMahon–Hussein correspondence] George Antonius, *The Arab Awakening* (Safety Harbor, Fl: Simon Publications, 2001), 419.

Page 46:   [McMahon quotation] "Report of a Committee Set up to Consider Certain Correspondence Between Sir Henry McMahon and he Sharif of Mecca in 1915 and 1916, Secretary of State for the Colonies," (London: March 16, 1939), accessed March 18, 2012, http://unispal.un.org/UNISPAL.NSF/0/4C4F7515DC39195185256CF7006F878C. *Note:* George Antonius was among the representatives of the Arab Delegation at these meetings.

ISRAEL-PALESTINE FOR CRITICAL THINKERS

Page 55: [cradle and home of their vital race] David Hunter Miller, "Document 246: Outline of Tentative Report and Recommendation Prepared by the Intelligence Section, In Accordance with Instructions for the President and the Plenipotentiaries, January 21,1919," in *My Diary at the Conference of Paris: With Documents* (NewYork, 1924), 4: 264. *Note:* David Hunter Miller was a member of the U.S. delegation at the Peace Conference and compiled a 21-volume diary.

Page 57: [We and they want the same thing] David Ben Gurion, JAG—Protocols of the Jewish Agency Directorate in the Central Zionist Archives (Jerusalem, May 19, 1936), quoted in Shabtai Teveth, *Ben-Gurion and the Palestinian Arabs: From Peace to War* (New York: Oxford University Press, 1985), 166.

Page 67: [war has its dark side] Benny Morris, "As Israelis Celebrate Independence and Palestinians Mark the "Nakba," a Debate with Benny Morris, Saree Makdisi, and Norman Finkelstein," Democracy Now!, 2008, accessed Dec 1, 2014, http://www.democracynow.org/

Page 70-71: [Nasser on the Strait of Tiran] Quoted in Jacques Paul Gauthier, *Sovereignty Over the Old City* of Jerusalem: A Study of the Historical, Religious, Political and Legal Aspect*s of the Question of the Old City*, Thèse No. 725 (Geneva: Université de Genève, 2007), 670.

Page 71: [Arab rhetoric] Quoted in Martin Gilbert, *The Routledge Atlas of the Arab-Israeli Conflict*, 9th ed. (London: Routledge, 2008), 66–67.

Page 73: [legislation] State of Israel, *Protection of Holy Places Law* 5727, June 27, 1967, http://www.knesset.gov.il/ laws/special/eng/HolyPlaces.htm.

Page 76: [Arab possession] Golda Meir, *My Life* (New York: Dell, 1975), 351.

Page 77: [definition of occupation] International Committee of the Red Cross (ICRC), "Contemporary challenges to IHL—Occupation: overview," accessed October 8, 2012, http://www.icrc.org/eng/war-and-law/contemporary- challenges-for-ihl/occupation/overview-occupation.htm

Page 77: [conditions for belligerent occupation] Alan Baker, ed., *Israel's Rights as a Nation-State in International Diplomacy* (Jerusalem: World Jewish Congress/Jerusalem Center for Public Affairs, 2011), http://jcpa.org/

Page 83: [on UN neutrality] Ilan Dunsky. "Israel, the Arabs and International Law: Whose Palestine Is It, Anyway?" *Dalhousie Journal of Legal Studies* 2 (1993)

Page 93: ["This is going to be a crime"] Elsa Walsh, "The Prince," *The New Yorker*, March 24, 2003, 58.

Page 95: [ICJ opinion on the security barrier] International Court of Justice, "Legal Consequences of the Construction of a Wall in the Occupied Palestinian Territory," Press Release 2004/28, July 9, 2004, http://www.icj-cij.org/docket/index.php ?pr=71&code=mwp&tp1=3&tp2=4&tp3=6&ca.

Page 95: [rights and entitlements] Jacques Paul Gauthier, *Sovereignty Over the Old City of Jerusalem: A Study of the Historical, Religious, Political and Legal Aspects of the Question of the Old City*, Thèse No. 725 (Geneva: Université de Genève, 2007), 781.

Page 101: [quotation in caption] Colonel Richard Kemp, UN Human Rights Council Debate on Goldstone Report, 12th Special Session, October 16, 2009. See Goldstone Gaza Report: Col. Richard Kemp Testifies at UN Emergency Session, YouTube, http://www.youtube.com/watch?v=NX6vyT8RzMo.

PART 3

Page 113: [Islam and Islamism] Maajid Nawaz, *Radical* (Connecticut: Lyons Press, 2013), 45–46.

WORKS/PERSONS CONSULTED

The list that follows is not intended to be a complete bibliography of all sources used.

Aharoni, Yohanan, Michael Avi-Yonah, Anson F. Rainey, and Ze'ev Safrai, *The MacMillan Bible Atlas*, 3rd ed. New York: Macmillan, 1993.

Antonius, George. *The Arab Awakening*. Safety Harbor, Fl: Simon Publications, 2001.

Avalon Project, *Palestinian National Charter, (as amended in 1968)*, Yale Law School, accessed March 25, 2012, http://avalon.law.yale.edu/20th_century/plo-cov.asp.

Avalon Project, *Mandate for Palestine*, Yale Law School, http://avalon.law.yale.edu/20th_century/palmanda.asp.

Avalon Project, Secretary of State for the Colonies, British White Paper of June 1922, Yale Law School, http://avalon.law.yale.edu/20th_century/brwh1922.asp.

Ali, Abdullah Yusuf. *The Holy Quran*. NewYork: Tahrike Tarsile Qu'ran Inc.,1934.

Baker, Alan, ed. *Israel's Rights as a Nation-State in International Diplomacy*. Jerusalem: World Jewish Congress / Jerusalem Center for Public Affairs, 2011), http://jcpa.org/wp-content/up- loads/2012/02/israels-rights-full-study.pdf.

Bass, Richard. *Israel in World Relations*. Toronto, 2013.

Ben Dov, Meir. *Historical Atlas of Jerusalem*. New York: Continuum, 2002.

Ben Sasson, H.H., ed. *A History of the Jewish People*. Cambridge: Harvard University Press, 1976

Bentwich, Norman. "Mandate Territories, Palestine and Mesopotamia (Iraq)." *British Yearbook of International Law 2* (1921–1922).

Bickerton, Ian J., and Carla L. Klausner. *A History of the Arab-Israeli Conflict*, 5th ed. Upper Saddle River: Pearson Prentice Hall, 2007.

Carroll, Robert, and Stephen Prickett, eds. *The Bible: Authorized King James Version* 2008. Oxford: Oxford University Press, 1997.

Dunsky, Ilan. "Israel, the Arabs and International Law: Whose Palestine Is It, Anyway?" *Dalhousie Journal of Legal Studies 2* (1993).

Freedom House, "Freedom in the World 2014," accessed December 1, 2014, https://freedomhouse.org/sites/default/files/FIW2014%20Booklet.pdf.

Gauthier, Jacques Paul. S*overeignty Over the Old City of Jerusalem: A Study of the Historical, Religious, Political and Legal Aspects of the Question of the Old City, Thèse No. 725.* Geneva: Université de Genève, 2007.

Gilbert, Martin. *The Routledge Atlas of the Arab-Israeli Conflict,* 9th ed. London: Routledge, 2008.

Gilbert, Martin. *The Routledge Historical Atlas of Jerusalem,* 4th ed. London: Routledge, 2008.

Gilder, George. *The Israel Test.* USA: Richard Vigilante Books, 2009.

Glick, Caroline. *The Israeli Solution.* New York: Crown Forum, 2014.

Grief, Howard. *The Legal Foundation and Borders of Israel under International Law.* Jerusalem: Mazo, 2008.

Johnson, Paul. *A History of Christianity.* Riverside: Simon and Schuster, 1976.

Johnson, Paul. *History of the Jews.* New York: Harper, 1987.

Kantor, Mattis. *The Jewish Timeline Ecncyclopedia.* Northvale NJ: Jason Aronson Inc., 1992.

Kedar, Mordechai. Correspondence with author. 2014.

Khalidi, Rashid. *Palestinian Identity.* New York: Columbia University Press, 2010.

Khatib, Hisham. *Palestine and Egypt Under the Ottomans.* London: Tauris Parke, 2003.

Lewis, Bernard. *The Middle East.* London: Phoenix, 2000.

Lewis, Bernard, and Buntzie Ellis-Churchill. *Islam: The Religion and the People.* New Jersey:Wharton School Publishing, 2009.

Luke, Sir Harry, and Edward Keith-Roach, eds. *The Handbook for Palestine.* London: MacMillan and Co., 1922.

MacMillan, Margaret. *Paris 1919—Six Months that Changed the World*. New York: Random House, 2003.

Morris, Benny. *Righteous Victims: A History of the Zionist-Arab Conflict*. New York: Vintage Books, 2001.

Nawaz, Maajid. *Radical*. Connecticut: Lyons Press, 2013.

Pappe, Ilan. *The Ethnic Cleansing of Palestine*. Oxford: Oneworld Publications, 2006.

Patai, Raphael. *The Arab Mind*. New York: Hatherleigh Press, 2002.

Piggott, Leanne. *The Arab-Israeli Conflict*. Merrickville NSW: Science Press, 2008.

Sachar, Howard. *A History of Israel from the Rise of Zionism to Our Time,* 3rd ed. New York: Alfred A. Knopf, 2010.

Said, Edward. *The Question of Palestine*. New York: Vintage Books, 1992.

Sand, Shlomo. *The Invention of the Jewish People*. Translated by Yael Lotan. London: Verso, 2009.

Scherman, Rabbi N., and Rabbi M. Zlotowitz, eds. *The Stone Edition Chumash*. New York: Mesorah Publications, 2000.

Spiro, Ken. *Crash Course in Jewish History*. Brooklyn: Targum Press, 2010.

Stein, Kenneth W. *The Land Question in Palestine*, 1917-1939. Chapel Hill, NC: The University of North Carolina Press, 1984.

Tuchman, Barbara. *The Bible and the Sword*. New York: Ballantine, 1984.

British Government, Secretary of State for the Colonies, *Report of a Committee Set up to Consider Certain Correspondence Between Sir Henry McMahon (His Majesty's High Commissioner in Egypt) and The Sharif of Mecca in 1915 and 1916 (London: March 16, 1939)* Accessed March 18, 2012. http://unispal.un-.org/UNISPAL.NSF/0/4C4F7515DC39195185256CF7006F878C.

Whitson, William. *The New Complete Works of Josephus*. Grand Rapids MI: Kregel, 1999.

CPSIA information can be obtained
at www.ICGtesting.com
Printed in the USA
BVOW05s1447040517

483141BV00019B/368/P